FIRST & Favorite
BIBLE LESSONS FOR PRESCHOOLERS

by Beth Rowland Wolf
and Bonnie Temple

Group
Loveland, Colorado

Dedication

"I will speak using stories... We have heard them and know them by what our ancestors have told us. We will not keep them from our children; we will tell those who come later about the praises of the Lord. We will tell about his power and the miracles he has done" (Psalm 78:2-4).

This book is lovingly dedicated to those who told me the story and to those who taught me to tell the story.

Beth Rowland Wolf

To the many precious children, past, present, and "yet to be born" who inspired these lessons; to my own children, Cara and Stephen, who provided so much playful inspiration; and to my husband, Chuck, my constant source of support and encouragement.

Bonnie T. Temple

First and Favorite Bible Lessons for Preschoolers

Copyright © 1996 Beth Rowland Wolf and Bonnie Temple

Visit our Web site: **www.group.com**

Credits
Authors: Beth Rowland Wolf and Bonnie T. Temple
Book Acquisitions Editor: Mike Nappa
Editor: Jennifer Root Wilger
Senior Editor: Lois Keffer
Chief Creative Officer: Joani Schultz
Copy Editor: Julie Meiklejohn
Art Director and Designer: Kari K. Monson
Cover Art Director: Helen Lannis
Computer Graphic Artist: Joyce Douglas
Cover Designer: Rich Martin
Cover Photographer: Craig DeMartino
Illustrator: Dana C. Regan
Production Manager: Ann Marie Gordon

Unless otherwise noted, Scriptures quoted from The Youth Bible, New Century Version, copyright © 1991 by Word Publishing, Dallas, Texas 75039. Used by permission.

Library of Congress Cataloging-in-Publication Data
Rowland Wolf, Beth, 1966–
    First and favorite Bible lessons for preschoolers / by Beth
Rowland Wolf and Bonnie Temple.
        p.   cm.
    ISBN 1-55945-614-0
    1. Christian education of preschool children. 2. Bible—Study and
teaching. I. Temple, Bonnie, 1952–   . II. Title.
BV1540.R65 1996
268' .432—dc20   96-16545
                                                                                            CIP

17 16 15 14   10 09 08
Printed in the United States of America.

Contents

Introduction

Congratulations! You've accepted the joyous and challenging task of teaching delightful, lively, fun-loving preschoolers! You're filled with anticipation...and perhaps trepidation. What should you teach? How should you teach it? And how much learning can you really expect from children whose attention spans are shorter than the time it takes to give an extra hug or wipe a runny nose?

Three- to five-year-olds are capable of learning more than many adults realize—especially if they're learning by doing. *First and Favorite Bible Lessons for Preschoolers* provides age-appropriate, hands-on activities that will teach young children important Bible truths. We've consulted with children's workers around the country and selected thirteen Bible stories that preschoolers will love and learn from. Although these stories are "old favorites" to teachers, most preschoolers will be hearing them for the very first time. You and your preschoolers will love these new and creative, yet entirely *practical,* Bible lessons.

The lessons in *First and Favorite Bible Lessons for Preschoolers* are carefully designed to appeal to all five senses. No matter how large or small your class may be, all of the children in your class will be actively involved in creative learning activities. They'll have lots of opportunities to practice working together and helping each other. In the process of completing these lessons, your preschoolers will discover the truths of Scripture for *themselves.*

Each first and favorite Bible lesson includes "God's Message"—a short, repeatable lesson "point." These points are quoted directly from Scripture, easy for children to understand, and easy for the teacher to repeat during each activity.

Preschool children feel happier and more secure when they have a familiar routine. So we've structured each first and favorite Bible lesson to include the following elements.

Sing-Along Start-Up—a new song set to a familiar tune for you to use to teach God's Message (The book also suggests additional songs to use for a longer singing time.)

The Bible Story—fun, interactive, and memorable presentations of Bible stories your preschoolers will love

Crafty Creations—age-appropriate, original craft ideas that are a snap to prepare

Classroom Specials—special games, affirmations, and other activities that will help children apply what they're learning to their lives

Snack Time—creative, fun-to-eat snacks that children can help prepare

Closing—creative prayers, songs, and other activities that will reinforce the important things children have learned

Use this resource to plan fun-filled, memorable Bible lessons for the preschoolers in your church. As you reach children with God's love, you'll be delighted to see preschoolers' faces light up as they discover "Jesus loves *me!*"

God Made It, and It Was Grrreat!

(Genesis 1:1–2:3)

♥ **God's Message:** "Everything God made is good."

(1 Timothy 4:4)

Young children are curious about the world they see. They wonder why it rains, why the sun shines, and how flowers grow. They are amazed by their bodies and delight in finding out how tall, strong, and fast they are. In today's lesson, you'll help children see that all creation is good because our Creator made it good.

This lesson will focus on the beauty and diversity of creation. The children will discover that God's creations are too numerous to list. They'll understand that God's creation is good and fun. They'll learn that people have been given the job of taking care of God's creation. And they'll find out that each of them is a special creation, created to do exciting things and to be a treasured member of God's kingdom.

♥ Preparation ♥

You'll need a Bible, water, a measuring cup, markers, a small plant, a stuffed animal, a baby doll, masking tape, and quick-hardening plaster of Paris (available at hobby or discount stores). You'll also need a resealable plastic bag for each child. Before class, measure one cup of plaster of Paris into each plastic bag.

For Snack Time, you'll need thin slices of white cheese, circle-shaped cookie cutters or plastic drinking glasses, and orange and apple slices (not wedges). Peel the orange slices, and cut the apples horizontally so that a star shape appears in the middle of each slice. (See illustration on page 13.) Remove all seeds from the fruit.

♥ The Lesson ♥

1. Sing-Along Start-Up
(up to 5 minutes)

For this activity, children need to see things that God has made. If there are no windows in your classroom, lead children to another room in your church that has a window or door to the outside.

Have children sit in a circle near the window or door. Say: **Let's talk about the things God has made. Look around the room and through the windows, and see what you can find that God has made.** Ask:

● **What did you see that God has made?**

Say: **God made all these things and many more. Let's sing a song about God's creation. When I point to something that God has made, call out what it is.**

Sing the following song to the tune of "Old MacDonald Had a Farm." When you come to the blanks in the song, point to something God has made, and have the children call out what it is. Sing the song several times so that children know the words and can sing with you.

Leader Tip

Ultimately, God is the Creator of everything, so accept all of the children's answers, even if they mention man-made items.

Everything God Made Is Good

Everything God made is good.
Let's give praise to God!
God made everything we see.
Let's give praise to God!
God made the _____.
God made the _____.
God made _____, and
You and me. *(Point to the children, then point to yourself.)*
Everything God made is good.
Let's give praise to God!

> If you'd like to extend your Sing-Along Start-Up time, sing "God Made Us All to Do Good Works" from page 32.

Say: **God has made so many things. And ♥ everything God made is good. Let's find out how God created the world.**

2. The Bible Story
(up to 10 minutes)

Open your Bible to Genesis 1:1–2:3, and show the passage to the children. Say: **The story of Creation is the first story in the Bible. Listen to the story about how God made the world.**

Before God created the world everything was dark. Shut your eyes to see what it was like. Then God created light. He made the sun, the moon, and the stars. Now open your eyes, and see God's wonderful light! God made the earth and the sky, too. The earth was solid and firm. Let's pat the floor to feel how solid it is. Above the earth was the air. Can you blow the air?

God put water in the oceans and seas. Let's gently move our arms like waves.

Then God made plants that grew and blew in the breeze. Let's wave our arms like plants in the breeze.

God put fish in the ocean. Let's wiggle our hands like swimming fish.

God put birds in the air. Can you flap your arms like a bird?

And God put animals everywhere. Make the sound of your favorite animal.

> **Leader Tip**
>
> Some young pre-schoolers may not be able to identify a favorite animal. You may want to suggest several different animals and lead children in making their sounds.

Pause for children to make their animal sounds, then continue: **Then God made people. First he made Adam, and then he made Eve. And then God made other people. Point to three other people in this room.**

God looked at the sun, the moon, the stars, the ocean, the plants, the birds, the animals, and the people, and God said, "It is good." ❤ **Everything God made is good. Let's all cheer for God. When I count to three, we'll all say, "Yea, God!" Ready? One, two, three. Yea, God!**

3. Crafty Creations
(up to 10 minutes)

Give each child a bag of plaster. Follow the directions on the package, and pour water into each bag. Close the bags, and help the children squish the water into the dry plaster. Have the children mold the plaster (with the bag still closed) into shapes they can hold through the plastic. In just a couple of minutes, the plaster will firm up. While the children are holding their plaster shapes, talk about the anticipation involved in their creation. Ask:
● **What do you think your creation will look like?**
● **Is it hard to wait for it to be ready? Why or why not?**
● **How do you think God felt when he was creating the world?**
When the creations have hardened, take them out of the plastic bags, and have the children decorate them with markers. Help children decide

what their new creations are. For example, their creations may resemble animals, plants, people, rocks, flowers, or mountains.

Say: **Each of your creations is different. No two creations are the same, just as no two people are the same. Your creations are special to you, just as the world is special to God. God cares about us, and he thinks each of us is special. That's because ♥ everything God made is good.**

Set the new creations aside to dry thoroughly.

---

4. Classroom Special
(up to 10 minutes)

Say: **Let's play a game called Adam Named the Animals to help us learn more about God's creation. God gave Adam the job of naming all the animals. Who would like to be Adam?**

Choose a child to be Adam, then continue: **In a minute, I'm going to ask our Adam to name some things that God has created. Adam will say, "Adam named the . . ." then name something that God has created. You'll have to listen carefully, because if Adam names an animal, your job will be to act like that animal and to make that animal's sound. If Adam names something that's not an animal, your job will be to stand still.**

Have Adam call out, "Adam named the . . ." and complete the sentence with animal names or other things, such as shirts, socks, or pencils. Be ready to help Adam think of different animals such as kangaroos, elephants, cats, dogs, mice, and lions. If the children aren't sure what an animal sounds like, help them make up a sound. Children who act out something that's not an animal aren't out of the game. Have them continue playing.

After Adam has mentioned several animals or objects, have him or her join the others, and choose a new Adam. Play for several minutes. Then have the children act out their favorite animals. Ask:

- **What animals do you like? Why?**
- **What animals do you see every day?**
- **What animals are in the zoo?**
- **What animals do we have for pets?**
- **Who made the animals?**
- **Why do you think God made animals?**

Say: **God made all of the animals, and he let Adam give them** names. God made many different kinds of animals. He made birds to fly in the sky, he made big animals such as elephants, and tiny animals such as mice. When God made the animals, he said they were good. 🖤 Everything God made is good.

---

5. Classroom Special
(up to 10 minutes)

You'll need a small plant, a stuffed animal, and a baby doll.

Have the children sit in a circle. Say: **God made everything.** Hold up the plant. **God made all the plants that grow on the earth.** Hold up the stuffed animal. **God made all of the animals that live on the earth.** Hold up the baby doll. **God made all of the babies and people who live on the earth. God has given people a special job to do, too. God wants us to take care of the things he created. Let's practice taking care of God's world right now.** Ask:

● **How can we take care of plants?**

Children may say, "Water them" or "Plant them outside in the sunshine." For each answer, pass around the plant, and have children pretend to complete that action. For example, have the children pretend to water the plant with an imaginary watering can. Then pass the plant around again, and have the children pretend to drop seeds into the pot. Then ask:

● **How can we take care of animals?**

Pass around the stuffed animal, and have the children pretend to take care of it in each of the ways they mention. Ask:

● **How can we take care of babies and people?**

Pass around the baby doll, and have the children pretend to take care of it in each of the ways they mention. Ask:

● **How do you feel when your parents take care of you?**

● **Who else takes care of you?**

Say: 🖤 **Everything God made is good. And God wants us to help take care of the things he made every day. God is pleased when we take care of his Creation.**

6. Snack Time
(up to 10 minutes)

You'll need thin slices of white cheese, circle-shaped cookie cutters or plastic drinking glasses, and orange and apple slices.

Have children make "moons" by cutting the cheese slices with the cookie cutters or glasses. Ask:

- **What hangs in the sky and looks like this?**
- **What does the moon do?**

As you hand out the orange slices, ask:

- **What is round and yellowish-orange and hangs in the sky?**
- **What does the sun do?**

As you hand out the apple slices, point to the star shape in the center of each slice, and ask:

- **What shape do you see in the middle of the apple slice?**
- **Where else do you see this shape?**

While children are eating, ask them to tell you about their favorite parts of God's creation.

When children finish, say: **God made the moon, the sun, and the stars. God made the sun to be a light for the daytime. The moon and the stars are small lights for the nighttime. God also made cheese, oranges, and apples so that we would have nutritious food to eat. All of these things are good because ♥ everything God made is good. Now let's thank God for one of his greatest creations.**

7. Closing

(up to 5 minutes)

Make a masking tape circle, square, or triangle on the floor. Make it big enough for the children to gather around it.

Say: **When God made us, he made us very special. God gave us amazing bodies. Let's thank God for making our bodies so wonderful.**

God gave us our feet to run and jump. Put your feet inside the shape, and say, "Thank you, God, for feet."

God gave us hands to wave hello. Put your hands inside the shape, and say, "Thank you, God, for hands."

God gave us ears to hear. Put your ear inside the shape, and say, "Thank you, God, for ears." Ask:

● **What else can we thank God for?**

When everyone has had a chance to thank God, pray: **God, we thank you for making us and our world so special. We know that everything God made is good. Thank you. Amen.**

Have everyone clap for God. Remind children to take home their creations.

The Rain Came Down, and the Flood Came Up

(Genesis 6:9–9:17)

💜 **God's Message:** "Look! It is the Lord God who helps me."

(Isaiah 50:9a)

Noah lived through a terrifying calamity of global proportions. But God took care of Noah and helped him prepare for the coming flood. God supplied Noah with the ability, knowledge, and materials to build an ark to carry him, his family, and the animals of the world safely through the flood until the earth became habitable again.

Like Noah, preschoolers face incredible challenges. They live in a world that's built on a grown-up scale. They can't reach the sink or the counter, yet they're expected to wash their hands. They want to dress themselves, but they can't reach the closet shelf or the top dresser drawer. And they're still learning basic concepts—such as numbers, letters, and colors—that grown-ups take for granted. The activities in this lesson will reassure children that God is always there to help them—even in scary or difficult situations.

♥ Preparation ♥

You'll need a Bible; six sturdy drinking glasses or Mason jars; six spoons; water; red, yellow, and blue liquid food-coloring; 1-foot strips of colored paper, such as construction paper, tissue paper, or colored bathroom tissue; markers; tape; a napkin or a paper towel; a CD or cassette player; and a CD or cassette of praise music. You'll also need half of a paper plate for each child.

For Snack Time, you'll need one-half cup of creamy peanut butter, three cups of sifted powdered sugar, one teaspoon of vanilla, and five to six tablespoons of milk. Before class, mix all the ingredients together to form a smooth dough. Divide the mixture into several small bowls. You'll also need a box of animal crackers and several plastic knives.

♥ The Lesson ♥

1. Sing-Along Start-Up
(up to 5 minutes)

Sit on the floor with the children. Say: **Today we're going to learn about how God helps us when we're scared.** Ask:

● **When do you get scared?**

Say: **Everybody gets scared sometimes—even big adults. Show me your best scary face.** Pause. **Wow—those are really scary faces! But I don't need to be scared, because God helps me. Let's learn a fun song to remind us that God helps us when we're scared.**

Sing the following song to the tune of "Pop! Goes the Weasel." Have the children follow your actions. Repeat the song until children know the words.

Look! It's God Who Helps Me

If you'd like to extend your song time, sing "Worship God" (p. 47) or "God Made Us All to Do Good Works" (p. 32).

When I am scared of bumps in the night *(cover your eyes and cower)*

Or feeling kind of lonely *(hug yourself)*,

I think of what the Bible says *(open your hands like a book)*:

"Look! It's God who helps me." *(Shield your eyes and look up.)*

Say: **When we get scared and need God's help, all we have to do is remember what the Bible says. ♥ It's the Lord God who helps me. Let's say that together. ♥ It's the Lord God who helps me. Now let's find out about a man and some animals who needed God's help.**

2. The Bible Story
(up to 10 minutes)

Fill six sturdy drinking glasses or Mason jars half full of water. Set the glasses in the middle of a table, then put a spoon in each glass. Set red, yellow, and blue liquid food-coloring on the table near the glasses. During the Bible story, children will create a jar of colored water for each color of the rainbow. You may need to adjust the food coloring to create blended colors such as orange, green, and purple.

Have the children sit around the table. Ask them not to touch the glasses until you tell them to.

Open your Bible to Genesis 6:9–9:17. Say: **Our Bible story comes from Genesis, the first book of the Bible.**

One day, God said to Noah: "You are the only good man on the whole earth. Everyone else is mean and bad. So I am going to send a flood to wash away all the bad things. I want you to build an ark—a big boat—for your family and for all the animals. You've been a good and faithful man, and I want you and your family to be safe during the flood.

So Noah hurried to build the ark. He gathered two of every kind of animal. Ask:

● **What animals came to live on the ark?**

All the animals crowded onto the ark. Let's scoot close together to see what that was like. Pause. **What do you think the ark sounded like with all those animals on board? When I say "ark," make the sound of your favorite animal. When I clap my hands, stop making your animal sounds. Ark.**

Allow a few moments for children to make their animal sounds, then clap your hands and continue: **Then Noah and his family got on the ark. Soon it began to rain. It rained and rained for forty days and forty nights. When it finally stopped raining, the whole earth was covered with water—even the tallest mountains. Everywhere Noah** looked, all he saw was water. But the animals were safe and dry inside the ark.

God remembered Noah, his family, and all the animals. God also remembered the earth before it had water on it. Let's talk about what God might have remembered.

Have a child put a few drops of yellow food-coloring into the first glass and stir. Ask:

● **What yellow things would God remember?**

Have the next child put a few drops of yellow and a few drops of red food-coloring into the next glass and stir. Ask:

● **What orange things would God remember?**

Have the next child put a few drops of red coloring into the third glass and stir. Ask:

● **What red things would God remember?**

Have the next child put a few drops of red coloring and a few drops of blue coloring into the next glass and stir. Ask:

● **What purple things would God remember?**

Have the next child put a few drops of blue coloring into the next glass and stir. Ask:

● **What blue things would God remember?**

Have the next child put a few drops of blue and a few drops of yellow coloring into the next glass and stir. Ask:

● **What green things would God remember?**

Say: **God remembered all the things he'd created. So he sent a wind to blow all the water away and dry out the earth. When the earth was dry, Noah, his family, and the animals got off the ark. God made a rainbow in the sky that looked like all of these colors.** (Indicate the colored water.) **God promised that there would never be another flood covering the entire world. And God promised to take care of Noah and his family. Noah thanked God for helping him. We're learning that 💜 It's the Lord God who helps us.**

Leader Tip

● If children have trouble thinking of specific-colored things God remembered, help them look for those colors in your classroom.

● If you have a large class, you may want to invite two or more children to help you with each food-coloring addition. One child can add the food coloring, and the other child can stir it into the water.

3. Crafty Creations

(up to 10 minutes)

Give each child a paper-plate half. Have the children decorate their plates with markers. Then invite children to choose several colored strips to tape to their plates in order to create rainbows.

Help children tape the paper strips to the curved side of the paper plate halves, as shown below.

While the children are working, mention that rainbows remind us that God loves us and takes care of us. Ask:

● **What other things remind us that God loves us?**

● **Is there anyone or anything that you take care of? Tell me about it.**

Say: **God helps us in many ways. He gives us good parents, teachers, and friends to take care of us. God also gives us ways to help others. We can hug our moms and dads and sisters and brothers. And we can feed, wash, and exercise our pets. ♥ It's the Lord God who helps us, and God is happy when we help each other. Let's play a game and see how God helps us.**

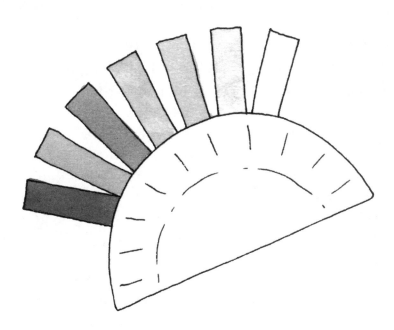

4. Classroom Special
(up to 10 minutes)

Say: **Noah and his family were in a scary flood. Big rainstorms can be kind of scary.** Ask:

● **What other things are scary?**

Choose one child to be It. Have It pretend to be one of the scary things children mentioned. For example, It might pretend to be a monster, a thunderstorm, or a barking dog. Give It a napkin or a paper towel.

Have children sit in a circle, and tell them to put one hand behind their backs. Say: (Name of child) **will pretend to be** (scary thing you've chosen). **If** (name) **puts the napkin in your hand, jump up and skip around the circle. Then It will sit down in your place, and you'll be It.**

Have It walk around the circle and act like something scary then drop the napkin in the hand of another child. Have the child with the napkin skip around the circle as It sits in his or her place. Then let the new child imitate something scary and drop the napkin in another child's hand. Play until most children have had a chance to be something scary. Then put the napkin away and ask:

● **What was it like to be the scary thing?**

● **What was it like to have a scary thing behind you?**

● **How does it feel to know that no matter what happens, God promises to take care of you and help you?**

Say: **This game was fun because we knew it was a game—the scary things couldn't really hurt us. Lots of things are scary, but God promises to help us and take care of us so we don't have to worry. That's why God sent a rainbow to Noah and his family. The rainbow showed that there would never again be a flood covering the whole earth. Now we all know that ❤ it's the Lord God who helps us. Let's see what else God can help us with.**

5. Classroom Special
(up to 10 minutes)

Have children stay seated in the circle. Say: **When you were a tiny** baby, you couldn't do very much except sleep and eat and cry. But now you're growing up and learning new things every day. God helps you learn things now that used to be too hard for you. Ask:

● **What can you do now that used to be too hard?**

If possible, have the children demonstrate what they can do. Some children may show that they can write their names, tie their shoes, skip, snap their fingers, or whistle. As each child demonstrates something, have the class respond by saying 💜 "Look! It's the Lord God who helps me." Encourage all the children to come up with an example. If a child has trouble thinking of something he or she can do, ask, "What can you do that a baby can't do?"

When all the children have shown a skill, say: **You can do lots of things now that you couldn't do when you were a baby. But there are many more things you'll learn to do as you grow up.** Ask:

● **What things will you learn to do as you grow up?**

Children may respond with ideas such as "read," "drive a car," "do math," or "ride a two-wheeled bike." Ask:

● **Who will help you learn to do all of these things?**

Say: **We have lots of people to help us. Moms, dads, grandmas, grandpas, sisters, brothers, aunts, and uncles all help us. But there's someone who helps us all the time. Remember, 💜 it's the Lord God who helps us. God promises to help us every day.**

6. Snack Time
(up to 10 minutes)

Have the children wash their hands and then sort animal crackers into piles—elephants in one pile, monkeys in another, and so on.

Provide plastic knives, and have the children each dab a small amount of the peanut butter mixture you prepared before class on top of an animal cracker. Then have them top the peanut butter mixture with a matching animal cracker. Have the children make two or three of these cookie "sandwiches." Have the children "walk" the animals two by two to their mouths, as they pretend their mouths are the doorway of the ark.

While the children are eating, ask:

● **Why did God keep the animals safe?**
● **Why do you think God helped Noah and his family?**
● **How does God help you?**

Say: **God helped Noah, his family, and the animals because God cared for them. God cares about us, too. That's why we can say,** 💜 **Look! It's the Lord God who helps me. Let's say it together.** 💜 **Look! It's the Lord God who helps me.**

Have children wash their hands and clean up the snack area before you continue the lesson.

7. Closing
(up to 5 minutes)

Give the children their rainbow plates.

Say: **I'm going to play some happy music because we're so happy that God helps us. When you hear the music, wave your rainbow up and down. When the music stops, hold your rainbow high over your head, and say,** 💜 **"Look! It's the Lord God who helps me."**

Turn on a cassette or CD of praise music, and let the children wave their rainbows. Every time you stop the music, have children hold their rainbows high and call out, 💜 "Look! It's the Lord God who helps me."

After two or three minutes, stop the music for the last time. Have children sit down and set their rainbows in their laps. Pray: **God, we thank you for taking care of Noah and his family. We thank you for taking care of all the animals. We thank you for taking care of our families, and we thank you for taking care of us. We know that you've promised to help us with everything we do. We love you. Amen.**

Remind children to take their rainbows home.

Moses Did What He Was Told

(Exodus 3:1–12:51)

♥ **God's Message:** "Obey the Lord your God."

(Deuteronomy 27:10a)

When God asked Moses to lead the Israelites out of Egypt, Moses had his doubts. What if he stumbled over his words? What if the king of Egypt wouldn't listen to him? What if the people wouldn't follow him? Moses could have let his doubts lead him into disobedience. But instead, he trusted and obeyed God's plan, and God helped him lead the people safely out of Egypt.

Like Moses, preschoolers have to trust and obey rules they may not fully understand. "Share toys." "Look both ways before crossing the street." "Wash your hands before you eat." Preschoolers' lives are filled with rules! Even though young children may not understand the reasons behind the rules, they fully understand that they can choose to obey or disobey. This lesson will show children that it's good to obey God, just as Moses did.

♥ Preparation ♥

You'll need a Bible, a puppet, newspaper, modeling clay, small strips of red and yellow tissue paper, and bowls of white glue. You'll also need a small paper cup and a twig for each child. Look for twigs that have several small branches.

For Snack Time, you'll need napkins, thin pretzel sticks, canned pineapple chunks, and banana slices. Before class, drain the pineapple chunks.

♥ The Lesson ♥

1. Sing-Along Start-Up
(up to 5 minutes)

Ask:

- **What rules do we have in our class?**
- **What rules do you follow at home?**
- **What's the hardest rule to obey?**

Say: **Let's sing a song about obeying rules. Be ready to tell me what the most important rule is.**

Sing the following song to the tune of "A Tiskit, A Tasket." Sing the song several times until the children know the words.

Obey the Lord Your God

> **Rules. Rules. They keep me safe and sound.**
> **But here's the most important rule:**
> **♥ Obey the Lord your God.**
> **Obey. Obey.**
> **Obey the Lord your God.**
> **Here's the most important rule:**
> **♥ Obey the Lord your God.**

Ask:

- **What's the most important rule?**
- **Who is supposed to obey God?**
- **Why is it important to obey God?**

Say: **God gives us rules because he loves us. Following God's rules helps keep us safe, and God is pleased when we obey.**

Today's story is about a man named Moses. Let's find out what happened when Moses obeyed God.

2. The Bible Story
(up to 10 minutes)

Open your Bible to Exodus 3–12, and show the passage to the children. Say: **God asked Moses to do something special. Moses could have said no, but Moses obeyed God. Your part in the story is to say, "Moses obeyed God." Say that with me: "Moses obeyed God." When I point to you, say your part. Ready? Here we go.**

For many years, Moses lived in the land of Midian and took care of sheep for his father-in-law. One day as Moses was watching over the sheep, he saw something very strange. A bush was on fire, but it didn't burn up. The bush burned brightly, but none of the other bushes nearby caught on fire. As Moses went to take a closer look, he heard someone say, "Moses, don't come any closer. Take off your shoes because this is holy ground."

The voice Moses heard belonged to God! Do you think Moses obeyed God? Moses could have walked closer to the bush, but (point to the children). **Moses could have refused to take off his shoes, but** (point to the children).

That's right. Moses obeyed God. He took off his shoes and didn't go any closer to the bush.

Then God said: "My people, the Israelites, have been slaves in Egypt for too long. I want you to go and ask the king to let them go free."

Moses said: "But God, I'm not very important. How can I go to talk to the king?"

God said, "I will be with you."

Moses was afraid to talk to the king. He could have stayed in the desert taking care of the sheep, but (point to the children).

That's right. Moses obeyed God. He went to Egypt and talked to the king. The king didn't want to let the Israelites go. But God helped Moses. He sent Moses' brother Aaron to help Moses talk to the king. Then God let terrible things happen to the king of Egypt and his people. So finally the king decided to let the Israelites go free. Because (point to the children), **the Israelites didn't have to be**

slaves anymore. They left Egypt and traveled to the land God had prepared for them. They were glad that (point to the children).

Ask:

- What good things happened because Moses obeyed God?
- What could have happened if Moses hadn't obeyed God?
- What happens when we obey God?

Say: **Moses found out that great things can happen when we obey God. Moses was scared to talk to the king of Egypt, but God helped him. God helps us when we obey, too. It's important to ♥ obey the Lord your God.**

3. Crafty Creations
(up to 10 minutes)

Cover a table or work area with newspaper. Give each child a twig with several small branches, a small paper cup, and a lump of modeling clay. Set out tissue paper strips and bowls of glue.

Say: **As you make this craft, you can practice obeying. Listen carefully so you can obey my instructions.**

First put the lump of modeling clay in your cup.

Then stick your twig into the modeling clay so that it stands up like a tree.

Next, dip a piece of tissue paper in the glue, and wrap it around one of the branches of your twig.

Keep gluing strips of tissue paper to the twig until it looks like a burning bush.

As the children are working, ask:

- **What might have happened if you didn't put any modeling clay in your cup?**

● **What might have happened if you didn't dip your tissue paper in the glue?**

● **Why is it important to follow the directions for this craft?**

When the children are finished, say: **You obeyed my instructions, and now you all have twigs that look like the burning bush that Moses saw! God used the burning bush to tell Moses about his plan. When Moses obeyed God's plan, a good thing happened—the king of Egypt let the Israelite slaves go free! It's important to ♥ obey the Lord your God.**

Have children wash their hands and clean up the craft area before you continue with the lesson.

4. Classroom Special
(up to 10 minutes)

Have the children stand in a circle for this musical game. Sing these words to eight successive notes in a scale. Each word is one step up the scale.

Toes
Ankles
Knees
Hips
Tummy
Shoulders
Nose
Head

To begin, sing the word "toes," and touch your toes. Then have the children repeat your word and action two or three times.

Then sing "toes, ankles" to the first two notes in the scale and touch your toes, then your ankles. Again, have the children repeat your words and your actions.

Continue up the scale, adding a new note with each word and having children repeat your words and actions.

Afterward, have the children sit down. Say: **Great job! That was a fun stretch. You needed to do a lot of listening and obeying in that activity.** Ask:

● **Did you think it was easy or hard to listen and obey? Why?**

> **Leader Tip**
>
> Preschool children love to sing and probably won't notice whether you can carry a tune. If you're uncomfortable with singing, simply speak the words instead of singing them.

● **When is it hard for you to obey?**

Say: **Thank you for listening carefully in the game we just played. It's important to listen carefully when parents and teachers give instructions. You need to listen carefully to God, too, because it's good to ♥ obey the Lord your God. Now let's talk about why we obey.**

5. Classroom Special
(up to 10 minutes)

Have children sit in a circle. Hold up a puppet. Have the puppet greet the children, then go through the following puppet script. Encourage children to help the puppet understand why it's important to have rules.

Teacher: (Name of puppet), **why don't you tell us about some of the rules you have at your house?**

Puppet: **We have lots and lots of rules at my house. My dad says that I have to pick up my toys before I go to bed. I think that's a silly rule, don't you?**

Teacher: **Maybe your dad wants you to pick up your toys at night so you don't trip on them when you wake up in the morning.**

Puppet: **Well, I guess that's a good idea. But let me tell you about another rule. I have to ask my mom before I eat a cookie from the cookie jar. What's good about that rule?**

Teacher: **Children, why is it a good idea to ask your mom or dad before you eat cookies?** Pause for children's responses.

Puppet: **I did eat too many cookies once, and I had a whopping stomachache. But what about all the rules for going outside? I have to look both ways before I cross the street and hold my babysitter's hand all the time. Why can't I just walk by myself?**

Teacher: **Children, why is it a good idea to hold a grown-up's hand when you're walking outside?** Pause for children's responses. **You see,** (name of puppet), **our parents give us rules because they love us and want to keep us safe. God's rules help keep us safe too. Children, can you name some rules that God wants us to follow?** Pause for children's responses.

Puppet: **OK, OK. I guess rules aren't that bad. I'll try to obey the rules at home and preschool this week. I want to stay safe. Will you obey the rules at your homes this week, too?**

Pause for children to answer, then say: **When we obey the rules, we stay safe and happy. When we disobey the rules, we displease our parents and God, and sometimes we even get hurt. It's important to obey our moms and dads, and it's important to ♥ obey the Lord your God.**

6. Snack Time
(up to 10 minutes)

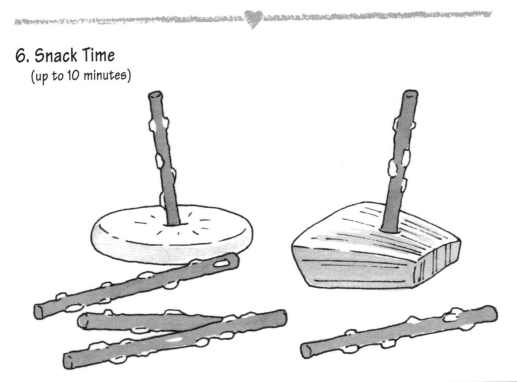

Give each child a few pretzel sticks, banana slices, and pineapple chunks on a napkin, but tell children to wait to begin eating.

Say: **As we eat our snack today, we'll practice obeying. Listen carefully, and do just as I say.**

Give the children instructions similar to these:

● **Eat one pretzel stick.**

● **Eat one banana slice.**

● **Pick up one pretzel stick, and poke it into one pineapple chunk. Then eat it.**

After giving several instructions, let children finish eating their pretzels and fruit. As they eat, remind them of the ways Moses obeyed God, and talk about ways they can obey God as Moses did. Point out that it's good to ♥ obey the Lord your God.

Leader Tip

If the children don't like an item, don't make them eat it. Give them different instructions. For example, you might say, "If you like bananas, poke one with a pretzel and eat it. If you don't like bananas, then poke a pineapple with a pretzel and eat it instead."

7. Closing

(up to 5 minutes)

Ask:

● **Who sets the rules that you follow?**

● **Why do they set rules for you?**

Say: **Our parents and teachers set rules because they love us and want to keep us safe. Let's sing our song about rules one more time. After we sing, we'll say a prayer to thank God for the people who give us rules.**

Lead children in singing "Obey the Lord Your God" (p. 24). Then pray: **God, we thank you for teachers and parents and other adults who keep us safe and sound with the rules they give us. Thank you, God, for giving us good rules in the Bible. Help us remember the most important rule:** 💜 **Obey the Lord your God.**

Remind children to take their burning bushes home.

The Boy and the Giant

(1 Samuel 17:1-52)

♥ **God's Message:** "God made us to do good works."

(Ephesians 2:10b)

Children love to hear stories that portray young people as smart, strong, and victorious. So it's no surprise that preschoolers love the story of David and Goliath. Good defeats evil as the young champion of Israel faces down a foe so fearsome that not a soldier in Saul's camp was willing to fight him. This lesson will assure children that God places no age limits on heroes of the faith!

It's unlikely that your children will be asked to slay giants or lead nations. Their special jobs might include sharing toys, helping with cleanup, or being kind to a new child at preschool. Use this lesson to help children realize that even as preschoolers they can play a special part in God's plan.

♥ Preparation ♥

You'll need a Bible, children's safety scissors, crayons or markers, colored paper, fabric and paper scraps, and glue. You'll also need a paper grocery bag for each child. Before class, cut out and discard the side panels of the grocery bags. Cut holes in the bottoms of the bags so children can fit them over their heads. Turn the bags inside out so the printing doesn't show, then draw a heart on the front and back panels of each bag.

For Snack Time, you'll need a seven-ounce package of vanilla wafers, three-fourths cup of grated coconut, three-fourths cup of powdered sugar, and one-half cup thawed orange juice concentrate. Before class, crush the vanilla wafers, and put the crumbs in a bowl.

♥ The Lesson ♥

1. Sing-Along Start-Up
(up to 5 minutes)

Sing the following song to the tune of "The Muffin Man." Sing the song several times until the children know it. Then have them suggest "good works" that God has made them to do. For example, a child might suggest, "Telling the truth." Then sing, "God made us to tell the truth…" Create a new verse for each child's idea.

God Made Us All to Do Good Works

♥ God made us all to do good works,
To do good works, to do good works.
♥ God made us all to do good works
And help our friends each day.

If you'd like to extend your song time, sing "Obey the Lord Your God," (p. 24) or "Love Your Neighbor" (p. 81).

Say: **Each person in this room is God's special creation. And ♥ God made us to do good works. That means that God gave each of us special things to do as no one else in the world can do them. God has great things planned for each one of you! Let's have fun listening to the story of one young boy who was given a job that no other man in Israel's army could do.**

2. The Bible Story
(up to 10 minutes)

Open your Bible to 1 Samuel 17. Say: **This is one of the first stories in the Bible about David. It happened when David was still a young boy. Later, when David grew up, he became the king of Israel. Today, let's find out what happened to him when he was a boy.**

Tell children the story of David and Goliath. You can read the story from an easy-to-understand translation or a children's Bible or tell it in your own words. Then have children perform this finger play with you.

Here is young David, so brave but small. *(Hold up your left index finger.)*

And here is Goliath, so mighty and tall. *(Hold up your right forearm.)*

Here is God's army, all shaking and scared *(wiggle all ten fingers)*

To see giant and boy so unevenly paired. *(Hold up your finger and your forearm.)*

David picked out five stones from the brook *(hold up five fingers),*

Then went back to Goliath and took a good look. *(Shield your eyes, and look up.)*

He put just one stone in his own leather sling *(hold up one finger)*

And threw it with skill and a flick and a fling. *(Pretend to wind up and fling a stone.)*

The stone hit Goliath's big head with a thud *(tap your head with your hand),*

And that big, scary giant fell down in the mud. *(Hold up your forearm, then drop it.)*

The soldiers all cheered, and they shouted "Hooray!" *(Cup your hands around your mouth.)*

"The Lord God helped David do good work today." *(Clap your hands.)*

Ask:
- **What was David's good work?**
- **How did God help David?**
- **What's a good work that you can do?**

Say: ♥ **God made us to do good works. David was just a boy,** but God helped him to kill a big, mean giant. God has good things planned for all of us to do, no matter how old or young we are!

3. Crafty Creations
(up to 10 minutes)

Say: **Let's make special shields like the ones worn by the soldiers in King Saul's army.**

Set out crayons or markers, and have children decorate the paper grocery bags you've prepared. Also provide colored paper, children's safety scissors, fabric and paper scraps, and glue. Show children how to cut or tear the colored paper and glue the pieces to the bag.

Have the children put on their decorated heart shields.

Say: **When David said he would fight the giant, Goliath, King Saul offered to let David wear his armor. But David didn't want to wear Saul's armor because it was too big for him. And even though David didn't wear any armor, he was still protected from Goliath.** Ask:

● **Who protected David from Goliath?**

Say: **That's right—God did! When God has a special job for us to do he helps us and protects us, just as he helped and protected David. Your heart shield can remind you that ♥ God made us to do good works and that God helps us.**

4. Classroom Special
(up to 10 minutes)

Say: **Let's march in a parade and pretend that these shields are our armor. We'll pretend that these heart shields are protecting us so that we can do good works for God.**

Lead the children in a parade around the room. As you march, sing the song "God Made Us All to Do Good Works" (p. 32).

Then stop and ask:

● **What special things did God want David to do?**

● **What special things do you think God wants you to do?**

Say: **Let's march again. Be ready, because when I hold up my hand, we'll stop marching and act out some of the special things God wants us to do.**

Leader Tip

If you have older preschoolers, let each child choose his or her own good work to act out. Or invite children to suggest good works for the whole class to act out.

March around the room, and sing the song. Then stop, and call out special actions for the children to act out. Include actions such as picking up toys, hugging a friend, or helping with the dishes.

Then ask:

● **When is it a good time to do the special things that God wants you to do?**

Say:  **God made us to do good works. God has already planned great things for us to do! And we know that God will help us and protect us. God wants us to be ready to do good works. Just as you had to be ready to do a good work when the parade stopped, we need to be ready all the time to do good works for God.**

5. Classroom Special
(up to 10 minutes)

Say: **God wants us to always be ready to do special things for him. Let's practice being ready and listening to what God wants us to do. When I call your name, be ready to do the special action I say.**

Have the children stand in a large circle so there's lots of room between them. Choose individual children from the circle, and have them perform one of the special actions listed below.

- Shake a hand.
- Rub a shoulder.
- Smile.
- Say, "You're special!"
- Pat someone on the back.
- Hug someone.
- Give someone a high five.
- Say, "God loves you."
- Link arms with someone, and spin in a gentle circle.

For example, you might say, "Charles, give Cassandra a handshake."

For the first few actions, wait for the child to return to his or her place in the circle before calling on another child. As children become used to the game, call out actions more quickly, so that several children are completing actions at the same time.

Repeat the actions as needed so that every child is called on several times to perform a kind act for another child. Clap your hands to end the game, then have children take three deep breaths and sit down. Ask:

- **How does it feel to do good works?**
- **How does it feel to have good works done for you?**

Say: **Some of you are still out of breath! You all did a super job of listening and quickly doing the special good works that I assigned to you. We need to listen to God and be ready to do what he has planned for us. When we do good works for others, we feel good, and they feel good too. That's because ♥ God made us to do good works.**

6. Snack Time
(up to 10 minutes)

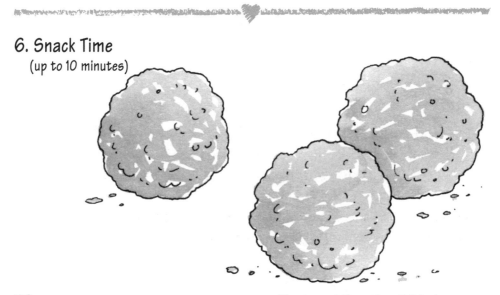

Set out the crushed vanilla wafers, grated coconut, powdered sugar, and thawed orange juice concentrate. Also set out an additional bowl of powdered sugar for children to roll their finished cookies in. Help children mix the ingredients together, roll the dough into small balls, and roll the balls in the additional powdered sugar. As children are working, mention that the cookies look like the stones David used. Ask:

- **How many stones did David use to fight Goliath?**
- **What did David do with the stones?**

Say: **David picked up five stones, but he needed only one. The first stone he threw hit Goliath in the head and made him fall.** Ask:

- **Have you ever tried to hit a target with a rock or a ball?**
- **Did you hit it the first time you threw?**
- **Why do you think David was able to hit Goliath with the first throw?**

Say: **David must have been a pretty good shot with his slingshot. He must have practiced a lot.** Ask:

- **What kinds of things do you practice to get good at?**

Say: ❤ **God made us to do good works. And God wants us to practice so we can be good at the things he asks us to do. We've practiced many good works in our class today. Before you eat your snack, pretend it's a stone like the one David used. Practice your windup as if you were going to throw the ball, but then instead of throwing it, eat it.**

Give each child two cookies. Then show the children how to wind up by moving your arm in a big circle two or three times before taking a bite out of one of the cookies.

Have children help you do the "good work" of cleaning up the work area before you continue.

7. Closing
(up to 5 minutes)

Say: **Let's thank God for the chance to do exciting things for him. When I point to you, I want you to name some good works you can do. You'll have to listen carefully to find out what kind of good works I'm thinking of.**

Have the children stand in a circle. Pray: **God, we know that ❤ you made us to do good works. Some good works are big, like . . .** Have children fill in the blank. **We can do some good works when we're small, like . . .** Have children fill in the blank. **We can do some good works when we're grown up, like . . .** Have children fill in the blank. **We know that you don't want us to wait until we're grown up to start doing good works. Just like David, we can start now, while we're still young. Help us remember to do good works every day. Amen.**

Remind children to take their heart shields home.

The Queen Who Served Her People

(Esther 1:1–8:17)

♥ **God's Message:** "Serve each other with love."

(Galatians 5:13b)

Generations of young children have been delighted by fairy tales such as Cinderella and Snow White. But the story of Esther is better than any fairy tale. Esther was a common-born orphan who, through an amazing set of circumstances, became a brave and beautiful queen. In a time when women were little more than possessions, the king took her word over that of his chief official. Queen Esther's selfless actions showed her devotion to her people and to her God—and saved the Jews from complete annihilation.

Preschoolers aren't in a position to influence royalty. However, Esther brings a message of devotion, humility, and service that everyone can learn from. Esther was the most exalted woman in the land. She could have used her position to save only herself. Instead she put her people's lives before her own. Use this lesson to teach your preschoolers that they can serve others as Esther did.

♥ Preparation ♥

Gather paper grocery bags; tape; scissors; glue; markers; and your choice of art items such as scraps of ribbon, yarn, or foil wrapping paper. You'll also need paper towels, spray bottles of glass cleaner, and a sheet of construction paper.

For Snack Time, you'll need three large bowls, paper cups, napkins or paper towels, juice, three small scoops, and three kinds of cereal.

♥ The Lesson ♥

1. Sing-Along Start-Up
(up to 5 minutes)

Sing the following song to the tune of "Frère Jacques." Have the children follow your actions. Sing the song several times so the children learn the words.

Serve Each Other With Love!

Serve each other *(point to other children),*
Serve each other *(point to other children)*
With love *(cross your arms over your chest),*
  With love. *(Cross your arms over your chest.)*
  With the words we say *(point to your mouth)*
  And things we do each day *(walk in place),*
  We serve with love. *(Hold your arms out, then cross them over your chest.)*
  We serve with love. *(Hold your arms out, then cross them over your chest.)*

If you'd like to extend your song time, sing "God Made Us All to Do Good Works" (p. 32).

After the song, say: **Our song is about serving each other with loving words and actions.** Ask:

● **What are some loving words you can say?**

● **What are some loving actions you can do?**

Say: **Today we're talking about kind, loving things that we can do for the people around us. Let's find out about a queen who served her people with love every day.**

2. The Bible Story
(up to 10 minutes)

Have the boys sit on one side of you and the girls on the other. Open your Bible to the book of Esther, and show the book to the children. Say: **The queen's story is found in the book of Esther in the Bible. In fact, the queen's name is Esther and the book was named after her! Listen carefully as I tell the story, because I have some actions for you to do. Boys, you'll be the king. Girls, you'll be the queen.**

One day before Esther became the queen, the king had a party. Boys, pretend to put on party hats. Pause. **The king told Queen Vashti to come to his party, but she said no. Girls, shake your heads.**

This made the king very angry. Boys, let me see your angriest faces. Pause.

The king decided to look for a new queen. He invited all of the most beautiful young women in the land to come to his palace. Servants arranged the girls' hair in pretty styles. Girls, pretend to brush your hair. Pause. **They put on makeup and sweet perfume. Girls, pretend to put on makeup and perfume.** Pause.

The king looked at all the girls. All the girls were lovely, but the king chose Esther to be the new queen. Girls, put on your crowns—Esther is the new queen! Pause. **The king loved Esther very much.**

The king had a lot of work to do to keep his huge kingdom running smoothly. He listened to his helpers. Boys, cup your hands around your ears as if you're listening. Pause. **The king wrote new laws to keep his people safe. Boys, pretend you're writing a new law.** Pause.

One day an evil man named Haman tricked the king and got him to sign a bad law. The law said that all the Jewish people would be killed. The king didn't know that Esther, the beautiful queen, was Jewish.

When Esther found out about the law, she told all of the Jewish people to pray and stop eating for three days. Girls, hold up three fingers for the three days. Pause.

At the end of the three days, Esther prepared a feast. Girls, let's pretend we're fixing a fancy dinner. What would you fix? Pause.

Esther invited the king and the evil man, Haman, to the feast. While they were eating, the king asked, "What do you want, Esther? I'll give you anything, even half of the kingdom."

Esther smiled and said, "Just come back tomorrow for another feast. Then I'll tell you what I want."

So the king and the evil Haman came back for another feast the next night. Again the king asked, "What is it you want, Esther?" Boys, let's ask the girls "What do you want?" Pause.

Queen Esther replied, "Please, my king, let my people live. They will soon be killed."

The king was angry that anyone would kill the queen's people. Let's see those angry faces again, boys. Pause. He said, "Who is the evil person responsible for this terrible thing?"

The queen pointed at Haman and said, "This is the man who wants to kill my people." So the king punished Haman, and Queen Esther and her people were safe. Esther's people shouted for joy. Let's all shout for joy and say, "Hooray!"

Ask:

● Why did Queen Esther invite the king and Haman to a feast?

● What did the king do when he found out that Haman was planning to kill Esther's people?

● How did Esther serve her people?

Say: Queen Esther asked the king to save her people. She served her people by saving them from an evil plan. Queen Esther was a brave queen who pleased God. ♥ God wants us to serve each other with love.

3. Crafty Creations
(up to 10 minutes)

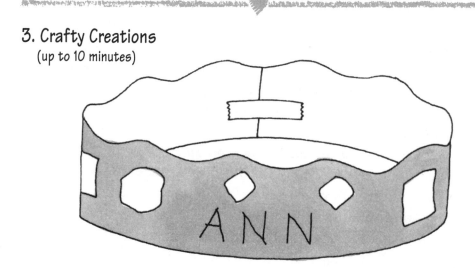

Before class, make a cut down one side of a grocery bag, and cut off the bottom. Fold the remaining part of the bag in half lengthwise, and cut off four-inch strips as shown in the margin. You'll need one strip for each child.

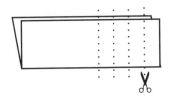

Set out the grocery-bag strips; glue; tape; markers; and scraps of ribbon, yarn, and wrapping paper.

Put a paper strip around each child's head, and mark the point where the strip needs to overlap in order to make a crown that fits snugly. Snip off the excess paper, and help children tape their crowns together.

Leader Tip

Older preschoolers may enjoy using children's safety scissors to cut points on their crowns.

Help children write their names on their crowns. Then have them decorate the crowns with markers and scraps of ribbon, yarn, and wrapping paper.

As the children are working, ask:

● **Who wears a crown?**

● **What do kings and queens do?**

● **How do kings and queens serve the people?**

Say: **Kings and queens have important jobs to do. They need to keep their people safe, make fair laws, and make sure people have food to eat and homes to live in. Kings and queens spend their lives serving other people. Put on your crowns to show that you can serve people, too. God wants us to ♥ serve each other with love. Let's talk about how to do that.**

4. Classroom Special
(up to 10 minutes)

Have the children wear their crowns as they form a circle and sit on the floor. Say: **Let's play a game of make-believe. We'll pretend that we really are queens and kings. Think about what you would do to serve people if you were a queen or a king.**

Go around the room, and have the children complete this sentence: "If I were a queen (or king), I'd…" Children may think of silly things such as "I'd make sure everyone had ice cream for breakfast every day." They may also think of serious things such as "I'd put all the bad people in jail."

When everyone has shared at least once, say: **None of us is really a king or queen—and we probably never will be. But there are important things we can do every day to serve people.** Ask:

● **What can you do to lovingly serve your friends and family?**

Go around the circle, and have the children mention their ideas. They may say things such as "Be nice to my new neighbor" or "Let my baby sister play with my stuffed animals."

When everyone has shared an idea, say: **We may not live in a royal palace like Queen Esther did, but we can serve people with love in the same way that she did. God is pleased when we**  **serve each other with love.**

5. Classroom Special
(up to 10 minutes)

Say: **Let's serve someone in our church right now. Our custodian works very hard to keep our room clean and pleasant for us. Let's serve our custodian with love by cleaning our room.**

Hand out paper towels and spray bottles of glass cleaner. Let children clean tables, doors, and walls.

Then print a note on construction paper that says, "Dear (custodian's name), today we learned to serve each other with love. We have cleaned our room to help you. Thank you for keeping our room so nice."

Have the children sign their names. Help those who haven't learned to write. Ask:

● **How does it feel to serve someone else?**

● **How do you think our custodian will feel when he (she) sees what we've done?**

Say: **When we serve others, everyone feels happy. God is pleased when we help each other. It's important to**  **serve each other with love.**

6. Snack Time
(up to 10 minutes)

Pour three kinds of cereal into three separate bowls. Put a small scoop in each bowl. Set two stacks of empty paper cups near the first bowl, as shown on page 45. Say: **Let's**  **serve each other with love by preparing a snack for everyone in our class to enjoy.**

Station children on both sides of the table. Have them take turns placing a scoop of cereal into a cup, then passing the cup along. When children have put all three cereals into the cups, have other children take the cups to your snack area. Have a few children set a napkin beside each cup of cereal.

When the snack is prepared, give children half-full cups of juice to drink as they eat their cereal. Ask:

● **How do you feel when someone does something nice for you?**

● **Who can tell me about a time someone served you with love?**

● **Who can tell me about a time you served someone with love?**

● **How does it feel to do something nice for someone else?**

Have children help clear the table. Then say: **Serving each other is a good thing to do. It makes everyone happy. The person we serve is happy, God is happy, and we feel good about ourselves. God wants us to ♥ serve each other with love.**

Leader Tip

If you don't have small scoops, use one-fourth cup measuring cups or smaller paper cups.

7. Closing
(up to 5 minutes)

Have the children wear their crowns and sit in a circle. Go around the circle and gently tap each child on the shoulder. Say: (Child's name), **you are an important person in God's kingdom. I give you the job of serving your friends and family.** Then have all the children say, "(Child's name), ♥ **serve others with love every day."**

When everyone has been "commissioned," pray: **God, we know you were pleased when Queen Esther served her people and saved them from being killed. We know that you want us to ♥ serve each other with love. Help us remember to do loving things for our friends and families every day. Amen.**

Leader Tip

If you have a twirler's baton, use it for a scepter in this activity.

Three Brave Men and a Wicked King

(Daniel 3:1-30)

♥ **God's Message:** "Worship...God and serve only him."
(Luke 4:8b)

Shadrach, Meshach, and Abednego held places of trust and influence in the Persian empire. But when they had to decide between bowing to the king's gods or remaining loyal to God and being thrown into a blazing furnace, it was no contest. God would be first in their lives no matter what. This dramatic story reminds us that God calls us to worship him and put him first. Putting God first is still a difficult challenge. Families, jobs, hobbies, and recreation can all vie for first place in our lives. But God asks that we worship only him.

It's not too early to instill a sense of worship in young children. Preschoolers already view the world with wonder and delight. As they come to recognize God as the maker of our big, bright, beautiful world, they'll see that God is as wonderful as his creation. And this is the essence of worship. Use this lesson to teach your children that one way to put God first in their lives is to worship him.

❤ **Preparation** ❤

You'll need a Bible; wax paper; newspapers; a dish towel; an iron; glue; scissors; and red, orange, and brown construction paper. Before class, cut out people shapes from the brown construction paper, using the pattern on page 54. Tear off two eight-inch wax paper squares for each child.

For Snack Time, you'll need graham crackers, chocolate chips, small marshmallows, teddy bear-shaped graham crackers, napkins, a cookie sheet, an oven, and a hot pad.

❤ **The Lesson** ❤

1. Sing-Along Start-Up
(up to 5 minutes)

Sing the following song to the tune of "This Old Man." Have the children follow your motions. Sing the song several times until the children know the words.

Worship God

> **Worship God.** *(Clap to the beat.)*
> **Serve him, too** *(clap to the beat)*,
> **For he's the only God that's true.** *(Hold up one finger.)*
> **He cares for us in many, many ways** *(hug yourself)*,
> **So we sing this song of praise.** *(Clap to the beat.)*

If you'd like to extend your song time, sing "The Lord Loves Us Very Much" (p. 90).

Say: **We come to church so we can learn about God and worship him. Worshiping God means telling God that we love him. The Bible says that we're supposed to ❤ worship God and serve only him. But one time, three men got in trouble for worshiping God. Let's find out what happened to them.**

2. The Bible Story
(up to 10 minutes)

Open your Bible to Daniel 3:1-30, and show the passage to the children. Say: **This story is from the Bible. Some very bad things and some very good things happen in this story. I want you to be ready for them. When a bad thing happens, let's boo together. I'll point my thumb down when it's time to boo. Let's try it right now.** Point your thumb down, and have the children boo with you.

When good things happen, we'll celebrate with a cheer. I'll point my thumb up when it's time to cheer. Let's try that. Point your thumb up, and have the children cheer with you.

Great! Now we're ready for the story.

There was a king whose name was Nebuchadnezzar. He didn't know about our God. He didn't understand that our God had created the world and everything in it. The king decided to make a statue and call it god. Point your thumb down.

We know that God isn't a statue. God lives in heaven. But King Nebuchadnezzar didn't know that. He told all the people that his golden statue was god. Then he told all the people to bow down in front of the statue and worship it. Point your thumb down.

But three men named Shadrach, Meshach, and Abednego knew better. Point your thumb up. **They knew that God isn't a statue. When the king said, "Bow down in front of this god," Shadrach, Meshach, and Abednego said, "No way!"** Point your thumb up.

This made the king very angry. He decided to punish Shadrach, Meshach, and Abednego for refusing to bow down to the statue. Point your thumb down.

The king had a furnace that was as big as a room. The king ordered his men to build a big fire in the furnace. It was so hot that no one could even get close to it without getting burned.

The king threw Shadrach, Meshach, and Abednego into the furnace. Point your thumb down.

But an amazing thing happened. The king threw three men into the furnace. Hold up three fingers. **But when the king looked into the furnace, he saw four men!** Hold up a fourth finger. **And the fire wasn't hurting any of the men at all!**

God had sent an angel to protect Shadrach, Meshach, and

Abednego from the fiery furnace. Point your thumb up.

When the king saw that the real God had protected the three men, he knew that he had been wrong. He told Shadrach, Meshach, and Abednego to come out of the furnace. The king promised them that he would worship only the true God from then on. Point your thumb up.

Ask:

● **Why is it silly to worship a statue?**

● **Do you think Shadrach, Meshach, and Abednego were scared to go against the king? Explain.**

Say: **The God who lives in heaven is the only true God. God made our world and everything in it—including us. He loves us very much. That's why it's important to worship God. Just like Shadrach, Meshach and Abednego, we should 💜 worship God and serve only him.**

3. Crafty Creations
(up to 10 minutes)

Plug in an iron, and put it on a table or counter where children cannot reach it.

Cover a table with newspaper. Give each child two sheets of wax paper and three people shapes cut from brown construction paper. Have children glue the people shapes to one sheet of wax paper. Then have them tear the red and orange construction paper into small bits and sprinkle the bits on top of the people shapes. Help children place their second sheet of wax paper on top.

One at a time, place the wax paper creations under a dish towel and press *only the edges* of the creations with the warm iron. Make sure the children stay a safe distance from the iron and the cord.

When the wax paper cools, the children can gently shake the pictures. The red and orange paper bits will move and look like flames, and the wax paper will crackle like a fire.

While the children are working, ask:

● **Why were Shadrach, Meshach, and Abednego put in a furnace?**

● **Why wouldn't they worship the king's statue?**

● **Why do we worship God?**

● **What things do we do to worship God?**

● **How do you think God feels when we worship him?**

● **How do you think God would feel if we didn't worship him or if we worshiped something else?**

Say: **God is great enough to save three men from burning up in a hot furnace. God is so great that he made you and me and everything we see. Our God is the only true God, so we ♥ worship God and serve only him.**

Be sure to unplug the iron.

4. Classroom Special
(up to 10 minutes)

Lead children on a worship walk. If it's a nice, sunny day, take the children outside for this activity. If it's cold or rainy, post pictures of God's creation around your room.

Say: **We worship God when we thank him for the good things he's made. Let's see what God has made. For the first part of our walk, look at the ground. What can you thank God for?**

Have the children call out their answers, such as grass, bugs, dirt, flowers, or puddles of water.

Pray: **God, for all the things you made that are on the ground, we give you thanks, and we worship you.**

Then say: **Now look up. What do you see that you can thank God for?**

Have the children look up as they walk and call out their answers such as the sky, birds, clouds, or heaven.

Pray: **God, for all the things you made that are in the sky, we give you thanks, and we worship you.**

Then say: **Now look all around you. What else do you see that** you can worship God for?

Have the children look around as they walk and call out their answers such as friends, trees, and teachers.

Pray: **God, for all the things you made that are around us, we give you thanks, and we worship you. Amen.**

Say: **God has made us and the world we live in. Thanking God for the world he's made is one way we can ♥ worship God and serve only him. But there are other ways to worship God. Let's see what it's like to worship God with our actions.**

5. Classroom Special
(up to 10 minutes)

Say: **We worship God when we obey him and do things that please him.** Ask:

- **How can we obey God?**
- **What kinds of actions please God?**

Children might mention things such as going to church, praying, singing to God, obeying their parents, cleaning their rooms, or picking up their toys. After the children have shared several ideas, have them stand in a circle and sing this song to the tune of "The Mulberry Bush."

> **This is the way we worship God,**
> **Worship God, worship God.**
> **This is the way we worship God**
> **When we . . .**

Have children raise their hands and name ways they can worship God. Choose one child's answer, and have the children act it out as they sing the verse again. For example, the children might pretend to wash dishes while they sing the first three lines of the song then fill in the last line with "wash the dishes."

Then choose another child's idea, and have the children act it out as they sing the song again. When every child has contributed an idea, say: **God is pleased when we obey him. Serving God and serving others is another way for us to worship God. It's important for us to ♥ worship God and serve only him.**

6. Snack Time
(up to 10 minutes)

Give each child one graham cracker, a few chocolate chips, a few small marshmallows, and two or three teddy bear-shaped graham crackers.

Have the children scatter the small marshmallows and the chocolate chips on their graham crackers then put the teddy bear-shaped graham crackers on top.

Carefully transfer the snacks onto a cookie sheet. Have an adult helper put the cookie sheet in the oven at 375 degrees for about five minutes. Watch carefully so the marshmallows don't burn. If an oven is not available at your church, use a microwave or toaster oven.

Carefully put each child's treat on a paper napkin. While the snacks are cooling, point out the difference between what happens to the chocolate chips and the small marshmallows and what happens to the teddy bear-shaped graham crackers. (The chocolate chips and marshmallows will melt, but the teddy bear-shaped graham crackers will look the same.)

As children eat their snacks, say: **The teddy bear-shaped graham crackers in our snack are like Shadrach, Meshach, and Abednego. They didn't burn up or melt in the hot oven. Shadrach, Meshach, and Abednego did what's right. They knew that it's important to ♥ worship God and serve only him. Because Shadrach, Meshach, and Abednego obeyed God, God protected them from the fire in the furnace.**

Leader Tip

If you have a large class, write each child's name on a strip of paper. Slip children's name-strips under the corners of their snacks to help you identify the snacks after they're cooked.

7. Closing
(up to 5 minutes)

Say: **The Bible says that we should worship God and serve only him. We worship God when we show God our love. Let's end our class today by loving and worshiping God.**

Explain to the children that when you wave your arms, they should clap and cheer. When you hold your arms tight to your chest, they should immediately be quiet. Practice a few times until the children follow your directions quickly.

Then say:

> **God is great!** *(Wave your arms while the children cheer. Then hold your arms to your chest.)*
> **God is good!** *(Wave your arms while the children cheer. Then hold your arms to your chest.)*
> **We will praise him, as we should!** *(Wave your arms while the children cheer. Then hold your arms to your chest.)*
> **Yeah, God!** *(Wave your arms while the children cheer. Then hold your arms to your chest.)*
> **Amen.**

Remind children to take home their wax paper creations.

People Pattern

God Is With Us!

(Luke 2:1-20)

♥ **God's Message:** "God is with us."

(Matthew 1:23b)

Most young children are fascinated by babies. They love to talk to them, touch them, and play with them. Children love to hear that Jesus was once a baby, delightful and small just as they were!

In this lesson, children will learn that Jesus was a very special baby—God's only Son, sent to be with us and help us. God sent Jesus not just to Mary and Joseph, but to people long ago, people today, and people who have yet to be born. Use this lesson to celebrate Jesus' birth any time of the year.

♥ Preparation ♥

You'll need a Bible, a flashlight, a copy of the "God Is With Us" handout (p. 63), poster board or stiff paper, gold or silver spray paint, scissors, a cookie sheet, rigatoni noodles, a hole punch, and masking tape. You'll also need an eighteen-inch length of colored yarn or ribbon and a sheet of colored construction paper or a carpet square for each child.

Before class, glue the "God Is With Us" handout to the poster board or stiff paper. Paint the poster board side with gold or silver spray paint. When the paint is dry, cut the puzzle apart then reassemble it on a cookie sheet with the picture-side up.

For Snack Time, you'll need one cup of peanut butter and approximately one cup of powdered sugar. Before class, mix the ingredients together to form a soft dough. If necessary, add extra powdered sugar until the dough is dry enough to handle. You'll also need wax paper and bowls of raisins, chocolate chips, slivered almonds, and coconut.

♥ The Lesson ♥

1. Sing-Along Start-Up
(up to 5 minutes)

Sing the following song to the tune of "Frère Jacques." Sing the song several times until children know the words.

God Is With Us

> If you'd like to extend your song time, sing "The Lord Loves Us Very Much" (p. 90).

♥ God is with us. God is with us.
Did you know? Did you know?
Jesus came to earth for us.
Jesus came to earth for us.
He loves us so. He loves us so.

Say: **God loves us so much that he sent his Son, Jesus, to be with us and help us. Jesus came to earth as a baby. When he grew up, he healed sick people, fed hungry people, and told people about God's love. Because Jesus came to earth, we know that** ♥ **God is with us. Let's bring out our Bible and find out how Jesus came to earth.**

2. The Bible Story
(up to 10 minutes)

Gather children around you. Open your Bible to Luke 2 and show the passage to the children. Say: **Today we're going to hear how Jesus was born. You can help me tell our Bible story. Some of you can be Mary and Joseph. Some of you can be shepherds, and some of you can be angels.**

Help children choose their parts, then reseat them so the children who are playing each part (Mary, Joseph, shepherds, and angels) are sitting together. Make sure at least one child is assigned to each part.

When children are in their groups say: **You can help me tell the Bible story by acting out your part. When I say "Mary," all the Marys and will stand up. If you're Mary, cradle your arms and pretend you're rocking a baby. Let's try it.** Pause. **That's very good!**

When I say Joseph, all of the Josephs will stand up and walk in place. Can you show me that now? Pause. **Very good!**

If you're a shepherd, stand up and put your hand over your eyes like you're looking far away when you hear me say "shepherds." Let's try that. Shepherds. Pause. **Good job!**

If you're an angel, stand up and flap your wings when you hear me say "angel." Let's try that. Pause. **Great! Is everyone ready to tell our Bible story?**

Read the following story. Pause after you read the underlined words, and prompt children to do their actions.

People had been waiting and waiting for a *very long* time. As a matter of fact, people had been waiting ever since the first man and woman had to leave God's special garden because they disobeyed God. They were waiting for God to keep his promise. God had promised to send them a Savior, someone who could make everything good and right again.

One day an <u>angel</u> spoke to a special girl named <u>Mary</u> and told her she would have a baby. Then the <u>angel</u> spoke to a special man named <u>Joseph,</u> who was going to be <u>Mary's</u> husband. The <u>angel</u> told <u>Joseph</u> that <u>Mary's</u> baby was special. He was God's Son, Jesus!

While <u>Mary</u> and <u>Joseph</u> were waiting for Jesus to be born, they had to go on a long trip. The ruler of the land had made a law that people had to go to their hometowns and write their names in a

special book so the leaders could count how many people there were. So <u>Joseph</u> and <u>Mary</u> had to travel to Bethlehem to be counted. That was far away for <u>Mary</u> and <u>Joseph.</u> There were no cars or airplanes. They had to walk all the way!

Finally they arrived in Bethlehem. <u>Mary</u> was ready to have her baby! But Bethlehem was so crowded they couldn't find a place to stay! Everywhere they went they were told, "There's *no room!*" Finally a kind innkeeper said they could stay in his stable.

And just in time, too! That night Jesus was born! <u>Mary</u> wrapped the baby with pieces of cloth and laid him in a manger to sleep.

On a hillside near Bethlehem, some <u>shepherds</u> were watching their sheep. It was a cold and dark night.

Have a helper turn off the room lights. Continue: **Suddenly an <u>angel</u> stood before the <u>shepherds.</u> Light shone everywhere, and it was beautiful.**

Shine a flashlight on the shepherds and angels. **The <u>shepherds</u> became very frightened. But the <u>angel</u> said to them, "Don't be afraid! I have good news. Today your Savior was born. He is wrapped in pieces of cloth and lying in a manger." Then lots of other <u>angels</u> joined them.**

All the <u>angels</u> joined the first <u>angel</u> and said, "Glory to God! Peace on earth to those who love God!" Can all you <u>angels</u> say, "Glory to God" Good job! **Then the <u>angels</u> left the <u>shepherds.</u>**

Have the angels sit down. Turn off the flashlight, and turn the room lights back on. Then say: **The <u>shepherds</u> said to each other, "Let's go to Bethlehem and find this baby!" So they did.**

The <u>shepherds</u> went quckly and found <u>Mary</u> and <u>Joseph</u> and the baby. The baby was lying in the manger, just as the <u>angel</u> had said. The <u>shepherds</u> told <u>Mary</u> and <u>Joseph</u> about the <u>angels.</u> After they had seen Jesus, the <u>shepherds</u> praised God because they knew that ♥ God is with us. Then they went back to their sheep, thanking God for everything they had seen and heard.

Have everyone sit down. Say: **Mary and Joseph, the shepherds, and the angels knew that God was with them. We can be happy too, because ♥ God is with us. He sent Jesus to us, and he'll never leave us. I have a special puzzle picture that will help us learn more about that.**

3. Crafty Creations
(up to 10 minutes)

Show children the puzzle you've prepared. Ask:
- **What do you see in this picture?**

Encourage children to point out Mary, Joseph, Jesus, the shepherds, and other details in the puzzle picture. Then say: ♥ **God is with us. God sent his Son, Jesus, to earth for us. When we believe in Jesus, we are all a part of God's family, just as these puzzle pieces are a part of one puzzle.**

Pull out one of the puzzle pieces, being careful not to let the children see the painted back. **If there's a piece missing, the puzzle isn't nice, is it? So just as all of the pieces are important to the puzzle, we're all important in God's family. We're each very special.**

Turn one of the pieces over, and show the children the shiny back. Punch a hole in the piece, then thread a ribbon through the hole. Tie a knot in the ribbon to create a necklace. Slip the necklace over your head. Show children the shiny side of the puzzle piece, and say: **I'm special because I'm me, all by myself.** Then turn the puzzle piece over to the picture side, and say: **But I'm also a special part of God's family.**

Let each child choose a piece of the puzzle and one of the ribbons. Punch holes in the puzzle pieces, and help children thread the ribbons through the holes. Set out rigatoni noodles, and let children add noodles to their necklaces. You may want to let children color the noodles with water-based markers.

As children work, remind them that ♥ God is with us. When children have finished their necklaces, tie knots in the ribbons, and help children hang the necklaces around their necks.

Leader Tip

- For a more festive look, spray paint the rigatoni noodles before class. Let the painted noodles dry completely, and supervise children closely to make sure they don't put the noodles in their mouths.

- If you have a large class, you'll need to create more than one puzzle.

- If you have time, set out crayons or markers and let children color the picture segments on their puzzle pieces. Then reassemble the puzzle before children make their necklaces.

4. Classroom Special
(up to 5 minutes)

Place sheets of colored construction paper or carpet squares on the floor around the room, one for each child.

Have each child sit down on one of the sheets of paper. Say: **I'm going to tap each of you on the shoulder and say either "wait" or "Jesus is born!" When you hear me say, "Jesus is born," everyone will jump up and move to a different sheet of paper. Remember, you have to wait until I say, "Jesus is born!"**

Play the game several times. Then say: **We don't have to wait for Jesus to come—he's here right now!** 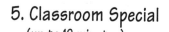 **God is with us!**

5. Classroom Special
(up to 12 minutes)

Leader Tip

If you have mostly younger preschoolers, you may want to place the tape line closer to where the children are standing.

Have children stand together on one side of the room. Place a line of masking tape on the floor several feet away from the children. Say: **Jesus is God's Son. When Jesus was born, everyone who loved him could say** 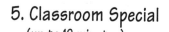 **"God is with us." Even though Jesus doesn't live on earth anymore, he's always here to help us. We're going to play a game and find out what it's like to have someone help us. When I say "go," hop on one foot to the line, then hop back. Do the best you can. Ready? Go!**

When everyone is back at the starting point, say: **Now find a partner, and we'll try something different.**

Help children find partners. Say: **The partner who's wearing the most blue will be the helper. The other partner will be the hopper.**

Help partners identify the helper and the hopper, then continue: **Helpers, you will help your hoppers by holding their hands and helping them hop across to the other side. Ready? Go!**

When everyone is back at the starting point, say: **Now change places with your partner. If you were a helper, now you get to hop. If you were a hopper, you'll be the helper now. Ready? Go!**

When everyone is back at the starting point, ask:

● **What was it like to hop by yourself?**

● **What was it like to hop with a helper?**

Say: **It's easier to do something that is hard when we have help. Because Jesus came to earth, ♥ God is with us. He'll always help us.**

6. Snack Time
(up to 10 minutes)

Set out small bowls of slivered almonds, raisins, chocolate chips, and coconut.

Have children wash their hands. Give each child a sheet of wax paper and some of the dough you prepared before class. Say: **Use your dough to make one of the characters from our story today. You could make Mary or Joseph or one of the shepherds or angels. Or maybe you'd like to make one of the sheep or another animal.**

Encourage children to use the raisins and chocolate chips to make mouths, noses, and eyes; the coconut for hair and sheep's wool; the almonds for wings, ears, and hoofs; and so on. As children work remind them that ♥ **God is with us. God sent Jesus to us, and Jesus will never leave us.**

When they have finished their figures, have children walk around the table and admire each other's work. Review details from the Bible story, then let children gobble up their creations.

7. Closing
(up to 8 minutes)

Say: **We've learned today that ♥ God is with us. When we believe in Jesus, we're joined to God's family. When I call your name, say ♥ "God is with us." Then come and hold my hand.**

We'll keep calling names and joining hands until we're all joined together. Then we'll march around and celebrate because we're all part of God's family. Ready?

Say: **Jesus came for** (name of child). Have that child answer, "God is with us," then hold your hand. Continue calling children in this manner until everyone is holding hands in a line.

While children are still holding hands, walk around the room as you sing the song, "God Is With Us," from the Sing-Along Start-Up.

♥ God is with us. God is with us.
Did you know? Did you know?
Jesus came to earth for us.
Jesus came to earth for us.
He loves us so. He loves us so.

As children leave, remind them to take their necklaces with them as reminders that God is with them.

God Is With Us

A Wild and Scary Ride

(Mark 4:35-41)

♥ **God's Message:** "I trust God, so I am not afraid."

(Psalm 56:4b)

One day during a terrible storm at sea, Jesus calmed the wind and waves and kept his friends from losing their ship and drowning. Jesus slept until they called on him; he wanted them to trust him. This story reminds us that Jesus is always with us and ready to help us. We simply need to bring our needs to him and call out to him for his help.

Young children have many fears—the dark, unfamiliar faces, big animals—just to name a few. Parents and teachers can help young children manage their fears by showing them that Jesus is their constant companion and protector. Even preschoolers aren't too young to learn to trust in God's love and protection. This lesson will encourage children to talk about their fears and ask for God's help.

💗 Preparation 💗

You'll need a Bible, a business-sized envelope, scissors, a marker, a stamp pad, paper plates, craft sticks, glue sticks, blue and green crayons, water-based markers, two small plastic margarine tubs, dried beans, and an old blanket or sheet.

For Snack Time, you'll need a knife, bananas, and bowls of small marshmallows and chocolate chips.

💗 The Lesson 💗

1. Sing-Along Start-Up
(up to 5 minutes)

Say: **Today we're going to hear about a time Jesus' friends were scared, then they learned that they could trust him. To help us get ready for that story, let's learn a song about trusting God.**

Sing the following song to the tune of "Ten Little Indians." Have the children follow your motions. Sing the song several times until children know the words.

I Trust God

💗 I trust God, so I'm not afraid.
I trust God, so I'm not afraid.
I trust God, so I'm not afraid.
Won't you trust him too?

Jesus will take care of us.
Jesus will take care of us.
Jesus will take care of us.
Won't you trust him too?

> If you'd like to extend your song time, sing "God Is With Us" (p. 56), or "Look! It's God Who Helps Me" (p. 16).

Say: **Jesus' friends trusted him to take care of them. Let's bring out our Bible and find out how Jesus took care of his friends during a storm.**

2. The Bible Story
(up to 10 minutes)

Set the business-sized envelope, scissors, marker, and stamp pad near you. Follow the instructions for cutting and stamping as you read the following story.

Open your Bible to Mark 4 and show the passage to the children. Say: **Our Bible story today comes from the book of Mark, and it's about a boat.** Cut the flap off the envelope and show it to the children. Say: **This will represent our boat.** Set the envelope in your lap.

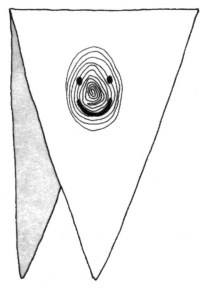

Fold the envelope flap in half widthwise. Using the stamp pad, make one thumb print on each side of the folded flap as shown above. Draw a happy face with a marker on each print as you say: **This story is also about something very special that Jesus did.**

Hold up the folded flap with the face prints, and say: **Jesus had been teaching all day by a lake. When evening came, Jesus said to his friends, "Let's go across the lake."**

Set the folded flap with the face prints aside, and pick up the envelope boat. Make a fingerprint on the inside of the envelope boat, and draw a happy face on it as you say: **So Jesus and his friends left the crowd that had been listening to Jesus and got into their small boat. See? I'm inside the boat. Let's get more of Jesus' friends in the boat.** Help children each make one fingerprint on the inside of the envelope. If time permits, draw a happy face on each print.

Hold the boat up for the children to see. Say: **Jesus' friends got into the boat. Let's all sit still now so we don't rock the boat! Jesus got into the boat too.** Tuck the folded flap with the face on it into the envelope.

Jesus was tired. He found a soft cushion and laid his head down. He wanted to rest a little bit while his friends rowed the boat.

Move the envelope boat gently back and forth, then say: **A breeze started to blow over the water.** Dip the envelope boat back and forth faster. **The breeze quickly turned into a big wind that blew harder and harder! Waves started splashing everywhere. Can you show me how you'd rock back and forth if you were in that boat?**

Have children rock back and forth, then continue: **Oh, the waves were so high! Pretty soon water was spilling over the sides of the boat. The waves were filling up the boat with water! Jesus' friends were scared. Jesus was asleep and wasn't helping! Can you show me a scared face? Yes, Jesus' friends were scared! They thought they were going to drown! Finally they couldn't stand it any longer. They shook Jesus and woke him up. They said, "Teacher, don't you care that we are drowning?"**

Jesus stood up. Stand up the flap in the envelope. Hold the flap steady as you keep rocking the envelope boat. **He looked out at the wind and waves and said, "Quiet! Be still!" Suddenly, the wind stopped. The waves stopped. And the boat stopped.**

Hold the boat still, and whisper: **It became completely calm.** Pause, then in a normal voice, say: **Jesus' friends were amazed—the storm had gone away!**

Jesus turned to his friends and said, "Why are you afraid? Don't you believe I care about you?" No one said a word. They looked at each other, then back at Jesus. It was very quiet in that boat. They didn't know what to say. Later on they asked each other: "Who is this man? He made the wind and the sea obey him! Only God can do that!" Then they knew that Jesus was very, very special—he was God's Son!

Put the envelope aside, and ask:

● **Why were Jesus' friends so afraid?**

● **Tell me about a time you were afraid.**

● **What did Jesus do to help his friends when they were afraid?**

Say: **Jesus' friends learned a lesson that day. They learned that Jesus is stronger than strong winds or waves. Jesus is stronger than big storms or anything else that scares us. And Jesus will** take care of us, just as he took care of his friends in the boat that day. Let's help each other by saying something that Jesus' friends learned: ♥ "I trust God, so I'm not afraid."

Have children repeat the verse together a few times before moving on to the next activity. If you have time and children are interested, repeat the song "I Trust God" (p. 65).

3. Crafty Creations
(up to 12 minutes)

Give each child a paper plate and three craft sticks. Set out blue and green crayons, and have children color their plates to look like sky and water. Older preschoolers will be able to hold a crayon on its side and rub, covering a larger area.

Help children glue their craft sticks side by side onto their plates to make a rectangular boat. The exact position of each child's boat on the plate is not important.

Cut a slit right above each child's boat, as shown above. As children work, say: **Jesus' friends were scared during the storm. But they learned to trust Jesus. I trust Jesus too. ♥ I trust God, so I'm not afraid. That's God's message for you and me.**

When the plates are completed, help children use water-based markers to draw happy or scared faces on each fingertip of one of their hands.

Show them how to stick their fingers through the slits in their plates so the faces on their fingers show.

Encourage children to pretend their fingers are Jesus' friends and to use their boats to retell the Bible story. Have them make rocking motions as they tell about the storm then tell the people in their boats, ♥ "I trust God, so I'm not afraid."

4. Classroom Special
(up to 10 minutes)

Put a handful of dried beans into each of two small plastic margarine tubs. Make sure each margarine tub contains about the same amount of beans.

Form two teams. Have teams form two lines about eight or ten feet away from you. Give the first person in each line a bowl of beans. Say: **Let's pretend that each bowl of beans is Jesus' boat with his friends in it. Your job is to get the boats to the other side of the lake. That's here, where I'm standing. I also need someone from each team to be a "rescuer." Your job will be to pick up any of the "people" that fall out of the boats and hold them until the game is over.**

Appoint a child or an adult helper to be the rescuer for each team. Then continue: **When I say "go," the two people holding the bean bowls will hop to me on one foot, then hop back to their teams and give the bowl of beans to the next person. Try not to spill any beans! If some of the beans spill out, keep going. We'll let the rescuer pick them up and hold them for us.**

Play the game until everyone has had a chance to carry a "boat" to you and back. Say: **What good boaters you are! It's a good thing we had a rescuer with us though. Lots of people fell out of the boat and needed to be picked up!**

Ask:

● **It would be scary to fall out of a boat. Who helps you when you're scared or in trouble?**

Say: **Like our rescuer, God helps us when we're in trouble. Let's remember what Jesus' friends learned and say it together:** ♥ **"I trust God, so I'm not afraid."**

> ### Leader Tip
> Hopping and keeping beans in the bowl may be too difficult for younger preschoolers. If so, have them take giant steps instead.

5. Classroom Special
(up to 8 minutes)

Spread an old blanket or sheet on the floor, and say: **To help us remember Jesus' friends in the boat, let's give each other boat rides around the room. When it's your turn, say, ♥ "I trust God, so I'm not afraid." Then we'll give you a ride.**

Let children take turns saying God's message then sitting alone or in pairs in the middle of the blanket or sheet. Have other children help you pull them gently around the room. Make sure everyone gets a turn. Then ask:

● **What was it like to ride around in the blanket boat?**

● **Did you trust the people who were pulling you? Why or why not?**

Say: **When you rode in the pretend boat, you had to trust the pullers to pull you gently so you wouldn't fall off. You had to trust the pullers to take good care of you, just as we trust God to take good care of us. Let's make yummy banana boats to help us remember to trust God.**

6. Snack Time
(up to 8 minutes)

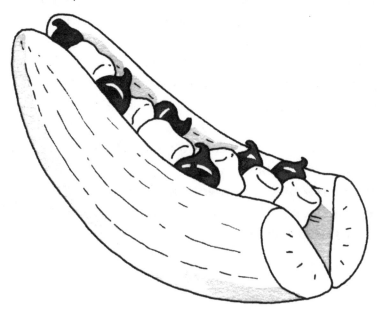

Cut unpeeled bananas in half widthwise, and give a half banana to each child. Have children peel their bananas as you explain that the bananas are going to be boats.

While children are peeling their bananas, set out bowls of small marshmallows and chocolate chips. Have an adult cut a lengthwise slit in each banana. Show children how to slip small marshmallows and chocolate chips into the slit. Explain that Jesus had twelve followers who were his closest friends. Help children count out any combination of twelve small marshmallows or chocolate chips and push them into the slits in their bananas.

Say: **Let's sail our boats through a pretend storm. As we're sailing our boats, let's remember to trust God.**

Have children "sail" their boats for a few moments then say together: 💜 "I trust God, so I'm not afraid." Then let children eat their boats.

7. Closing
(up to 5 minutes)

Gather the children, and sit with them on the floor. Distribute the paper-plate boats children made during Crafty Creations. Say: **Before we put our finger people in our boats, can you help me think of a time we can remember to trust God and not be afraid?**

Children may suggest fearful times such as thunderstorms; going to bed in a dark room; or meeting a big, barking dog. Repeat each child's suggestion, saying something like: "Yes, we can trust God and not be afraid when there's a thunderstorm."

When a child names a time to trust God, have children put one finger in their boats and say 💜 "I trust God, so I'm not afraid."

Continue until children have all their fingers of one hand in their boats. Then say: **Let's pray and thank God for always being with us. Thank you, God, for loving us. Thank you for always taking care of us. Help us to trust you. Amen.**

Give children an opportunity to pray if they want to. Remind them to take their boats home. Encourage them to use the boats to tell their families about Jesus calming the storm.

Never Too Little

(Mark 10:13-16)

💜 **God's Message:** "Let the little children come to me."

(Mark 10:14a)

Most young children have grown-up friends they love to be around. They usually aren't content to observe their grown-up friends from a distance; they want to run up to them, hug them, and play with them. Most adults welcome the openness, warmth, and eagerness of children. But Jesus' disciples didn't appreciate the presence of children when parents brought them to Jesus to be blessed. They saw the children as a nuisance and rebuked the parents. Imagine their surprise when Jesus not only welcomed the children, but exhorted his followers to be like them!

Preschoolers' self-esteem rises dramatically when the adults in their lives acknowledge them with hugs, playfulness, and laughter. Just as Jesus welcomed the little children who came to see him, he welcomes each child in your class. Enjoy this lesson as children learn that Jesus loves them and is never too busy for them.

♥ Preparation ♥

You'll need a Bible, scissors, a variety of textured materials (such as corrugated cardboard, sandpaper, needlework canvas, or textured wallpaper), white paper, and jumbo-sized crayons with the wrappers removed. Before class, cut different-sized heart shapes out of the textured materials. Make the hearts large enough for children to handle easily.

For Snack Time, you'll need the following ingredients for every four or five children: one cup of milk, one banana, one-half cup of fresh or frozen strawberries, one tablespoon of honey, and one-third cup of plain or strawberry yogurt. You'll also need a blender, bowls, measuring cups, measuring spoons, paper cups, drinking straws, construction paper, and scissors.

Before class, place each ingredient in a separate bowl. Cut out a small construction paper heart for each child. Cut two slits in each heart so that a drinking straw can be slipped through it (see diagram on page 77 .

♥ The Lesson ♥

1. Sing-Along Start-Up
(up to 5 minutes)

Say: **Today we're going to learn about a special friend who loves us very much. Can you guess who it is?**

Let children guess, then continue: **Our special friend is Jesus, and today we're going to hear how much Jesus loves little children. Let's sing a song about that.**

Sing the following song to the tune of "Frère Jacques." Have the children follow your motions. Sing the song several times until children know the words.

♫ Jesus Loves the Children ♫

♥ **"Let the children come to me"** *(beckon toward yourself)*,
Jesus says, Jesus says. *(Point to your mouth.)*
"I love little children." *(Hug yourself.)*
"Let them come to me" *(beckon toward yourself)*,
Jesus says, Jesus says. *(Point to your mouth.)*

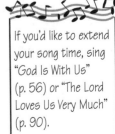

If you'd like to extend your song time, sing "God Is With Us" (p. 56) or "The Lord Loves Us Very Much" (p. 90).

2. The Bible Story

(up to 10 minutes)

Open your Bible to Mark 10, and show the passage to the children. Ask:

● **Do you have a special aunt or uncle or grown-up friend you love to be around? Tell me about your favorite adult.**

Give children time to respond, then continue: **When you love someone, you want to be with that person. That's how some children felt about Jesus in our Bible story today. You can help me tell the Bible story. When I say "Jesus," I'll cup my hand around my ear. When you see me do that, you will say, "Jesus, Jesus!" Let's try that. Jesus.** Pause for children's response. **Good job!** Read the following story. Each time you say "Jesus," cup your hand around your ear and wait for children to respond.

One day some moms and dads decided to take their children to Jesus. They wanted Jesus to hold their children and talk to them. The children wanted to see Jesus too. They were all very excited and happy as they made their way toward Jesus through a crowd of people. But as the children got closer to Jesus, his grown-up followers stopped them. "Don't you see that Jesus is busy?" they scolded. "He doesn't have time for little kids!"

Ask:

● **How do you think those children felt when they heard that?**

● **Can you think of a time a parent or grown-up friend was too busy to play with you? Tell me about it.**

Continue: **Well, the parents and the children were surprised when Jesus' friends told them to go away. They felt sad. They had gotten so close to Jesus. One or two of the littlest children began to cry. Can you show me how you would cry?** Pause.

Just then Jesus saw what was going on. He was upset with his followers for telling the children to go away. Of course he wanted to see the children! They were important to him! Jesus said:

♥ **"Let the little children come to me. Don't stop them. They are important. My father's kingdom belongs to children like these. You should be like them." Then Jesus took the children in his arms, put his hands on them, and blessed them.**

Ask:

● **What would it be like to get a hug from Jesus?**

● **What would you say to Jesus if he hugged you?**

Say: **Let's pretend we really are the children who were with Jesus and act out our Bible story now. If you're wearing something green, stand up.** Wait for children wearing green to stand, then say: **You will be the children in our story. Stand behind everyone else.**

Wait for children to move behind the group, then continue: **Everyone who is sitting down is one of Jesus' followers. You will block the way between the children and me. When I say, "Jesus is here," the children will try to come toward me. The rest of you will stand in their way and say, "Jesus is too busy." Let me hear you say that.**

Let children practice their lines, then continue: **When I say, ♥ "Let the little children come to me," let the children through. Children, when you get to me, I'll give you each a big hug. Then we'll trade jobs, and the followers can become the children.**

Say: **Jesus is here,** and have the followers stand in the way. After a few moments, say: **Let the children come to me,** and encourage the followers to let the children through. Repeat the story until all the children have had a turn being a child and receiving a hug.

3. Crafty Creations
(up to 10 minutes)

Set out jumbo-sized crayons and the textured hearts you prepared before class. Let each child take two sheets of white paper and two or three textured hearts. Help children arrange the hearts on one sheet of paper then lay the second sheet of paper on top of the hearts. Show them how to rub over the textured hearts with the crayons. Older preschoolers will be able to rub using the sides of the crayons.

As children work, remind them that Jesus loves children. Encourage them to repeat God's message with you: ♥ **Let the little children come to me.**

4. Classroom Special
(up to 5 minutes)

Leader Tip

Older children may want to sing the answer by themselves. You can have them sing alone, "Here I am," instead of having everyone sing, "Here she (he) is."

Sing the song introduced during the Sing-Along Start-Up. Then add the following verse. Sing the questions, and encourage children to sing the answers with you. As children sing, have them point to the child you've named.

Teacher: **Where is** (name of child)**? Where is** (name)**?**
Children: **Here she** (he) **is! Here she** (he) **is!**
Teacher: **Who loves her** (him) **so much? Who loves her** (him) **so much?**
Children: **Jesus does. Jesus does.**

Be sure to sing each child's name. When you finish the song, say: **Jesus loves us. No matter how big or little we are, Jesus says,** ♥ **"Let the little children come to me."**

5. Classroom Special
(up to 10 minutes)

Stand near the light switch, and gather the children around you. Say: **After Jesus said,** ♥ **"Let the little children come to me," he held the children and hugged them. Let's play a fun game of Hug Tag. I'll tell you how to move around the room. When I turn off the lights, give the person closest to you a gentle hug. Is everyone ready? Take lots of giant steps, and move around the room.**

Give children time to take several giant steps. Then turn off the lights and say: **Hug tag! Gently hug the person closest to you!**

Give other movement directions such as "take heel-to-toe steps," "twirl around the room," "jump," "scoot on your bottom," and "crawl on your hands and knees." After you give each instruction, allow time for children to follow it, then turn off the lights and have them hug each other.

End the game by saying: **Jesus says, ♥ "Let the little children come to me." Let's have one big group hug together. Jesus loves us all so much!**

6. Snack Time
(up to 12 minutes)

Set out the bowls of ingredients, the paper hearts, the paper cups, and the drinking straws.

Set the blender base on a counter or table away from the area where children will be working. Set the blender pitcher near the ingredients in the children's work area. Set appropriate measuring cups and spoons near each bowl so children can measure the ingredients for each batch of drinks.

Say: **Jesus says, ♥ "Let the little children come to me." I'm glad Jesus loves children. Are you glad? Let's celebrate Jesus' love with a special strawberry surprise!**

Hold up a straw and one of the paper hearts with slits, and say: **Everyone can help with our celebration. Some of you can make special heart straws like this.**

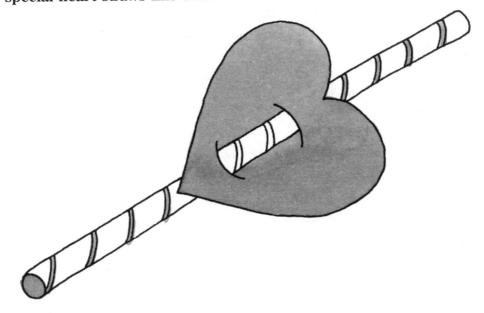

Demonstrate how to slip the straw through the heart, as shown on page 77. **Some of you can help make our strawberry surprise, and others can help serve it.**

While some children are assembling the straws, help other children measure the ingredients and pour them into the blender pitcher. For each batch, you'll need one cup of milk, one banana, one-half cup of fresh or frozen strawberries, one tablespoon of honey, and one-third cup of plain or strawberry yogurt.

When children have assembled the ingredients for one batch, put the lid on the blender pitcher and have an adult blend the drink at a safe distance from the children. Help children pour the drink into paper cups. Continue mixing batches until you've prepared enough for each child to have some. Have the serving group pass out a strawberry surprise and a straw to everyone. Thank Jesus for his love, then enjoy the strawberry surprise!

Have children throw their cups away and help clean up any mess before you move on to the closing activity.

7. Closing
(up to 5 minutes)

Gather the children in a circle. Hold up one of the textured hearts from Crafty Creations. Say: **Jesus says, ♥ "Let the little children come to me." That means he loves you! Let's pass this heart shape around the circle and tell each other, "Jesus loves you."**

Pass the heart to the child next to you, and have everyone say together, "Jesus loves (name of child)." Have that child pass the heart to the next child. Continue around the circle until each child has been affirmed.

Remind children to take their textured-heart pictures home.

Good Neighbors

(Luke 10:25-37)

♥ **God's Message:** "Love the Lord...and love your neighbor as yourself."

(Luke 10:27)

Jesus' powerful story of a Samaritan who helped a wounded robbery victim holds important lessons for us all. The Jews of Jesus' time scorned Samaritans. So when Jesus chose a Samaritan as the hero of his story and portrayed a priest and a Levite as uncaring passersby, he struck a stinging blow to the self-righteous teacher of the law who had opened the debate. The fact is, all of us are quicker to offer help to familiar people than to strangers or to those who come from backgrounds different from ours. Jesus' teaching makes it clear that, when it's in our power to do so, God wants us to show kindness and compassion to anyone who needs it.

Kindness doesn't come easily to preschoolers. They'd rather keep all the blocks for themselves than share with a friend. They'd rather go first all the time than wait their turn. Knowing that God wants them to be helpful and kind can help them make right choices as they play together. Use this lesson to encourage children to be loving and helpful to those around them.

♥ Preparation ♥

You'll need a Bible, a resealable plastic bag or paper lunch sack for each child, a variety of Band-Aids, cotton balls, stickers, and a permanent marker. Before class, make a sample first-aid kit by placing two or three Band-Aids, a few cotton balls, and several stickers into one of the bags. Decorate the outside of the bag with a few stickers.

You'll also need two long ropes, a sheet or blanket, several throw pillows, five or six carpet squares or sheets of construction paper, a small pillow, a stuffed animal, an umbrella, a drinking cup, a coloring book, and crayons.

For Snack Time, you'll need a bag of sliced bread, plastic knives, two jars or bowls of peanut butter, paper plates, cups, and a pitcher of juice or water. Before class, remove half of the bread, and put it in another bag.

♥ The Lesson ♥

1. Sing-Along Start-Up
(up to 5 minutes)

Say: **Today you'll be learning to ♥ love the Lord . . . and love your neighbor as you love yourself. Let's see what it's like to love ourselves.**

Read the following instructions, one at a time. Pause after you read each one so that children can complete the action.

- **Stand up if you've eaten today.**
- **Sit down if you went to sleep last night.**
- **Pat your head if you combed or brushed your hair today.**
- **Clap your hands if you're wearing clothes.**

Say: **One way we show we love ourselves is by taking care of our bodies. We eat, sleep, comb our hair, and get dressed every day. Today we're going to find out how we can show that we love others. We may not take care of others exactly the same way we take care of ourselves, but God wants us to love others as much as we love ourselves. Let's sing a song about that.**

Sing the following song to the tune of "Frère Jacques." Sing the song several times until children know the words.

Love Your Neighbor

Love the Lord,
And love your neighbor
As yourself, as yourself.
Love the Lord first,
Then your neighbor next.
Jesus says, Jesus says.

> If you'd like to extend your song time, sing "God Made Us All to Do Good Works" (p. 32) or "Serve Each Other With Love" (p. 40).

2. The Bible Story
(up to 8 minutes)

Open your Bible to Luke 10, and show the passage to the children. Say: **One day a man said to Jesus, ♥ "I know I should love the Lord and love my neighbor as myself. But who is my neighbor?" Jesus answered the man's question by telling a story. You can help tell the story by standing up and doing what I do.**

Have younger preschoolers do the motions with you while you tell the story. Older preschoolers can both do the motions and repeat the words after you.

Say	Do
Hi! I'm the man in Jesus' story!	Wave, and point to yourself with your thumb.
One day I had to travel to another town.	Walk in place.
On the way, a scary thing happened to me.	Hug yourself and shiver.
Some robbers attacked me.	Shield your face.
They tore my clothes.	Pretend to tear your clothes.
They took my money and beat me up.	Pound your chest, then kneel down.
Then they left me by the side of the road.	Lay your head on your hands.
A Jewish priest walked by.	Stand up, and walk in place.
He could see that I was hurt.	Shield your eyes with your hand.
But he didn't help me.	Shake your head and shrug.

Then another man came by.	Walk in place.
He took a good look at me.	Shield your eyes with your hand.
Then he walked away too!	Walk in place.
I thought for sure I was going to die.	Cover your face with your hands, and shake your head.
Then a man from Samaria walked over.	Walk in place.
People from Samaria are supposed to be my enemies.	Continue walking in place, and punch your fists in the air.
But he stopped to help me!	Stop walking.
He put medicine on my hurts.	Pat your arms and legs.
Then he put me on his own donkey.	Hold two fingers up for ears, then lay your other hand across the first hand.
He took me to a place where I could rest and get well.	Move your arm as if the "donkey" is walking.
He took care of me.	Gently stroke your cheek.
He paid for everything I needed.	Pretend to hand coins to someone.
I finally got better.	Hold your arms out, palms up.
After Jesus told my story, he asked, "Which man was a true neighbor?"	Point to your head as if you're thinking.
That's easy for me to answer!	Point your thumb to yourself.
The good neighbor is the one who helped me!	Hug yourself.
Jesus said we should be like the good neighbor.	Clasp your hands together.
I'm going to do that!	Nod your head yes.
Will you?	Point to the children.

Have children sit down, and ask:

● **What did the first two people do when they walked by the man who was hurt?**

● **How do you think the hurt man felt when they didn't help him?**

● **Who was the good neighbor in our story?**

● **Did you ever help someone? Tell me about it.**

Say: **God is pleased when we help others as the good neighbor in** our story did. God wants you to  love the Lord and love your neighbor as yourself. Let's have fun making something we can use to help others.

3. Crafty Creations
(up to 10 minutes)

Say: **The man in our story needed someone to bandage up his cuts and scrapes. Tell me about a time you needed a Band-Aid.**

Give children time to respond. Then say: **It's good to have Band-Aids on hand in case someone gets a scrape or cut. Let's use Band-Aids and some other things to make first-aid kits. Then we'll be ready to help someone who's hurt.**

Hold up the sample first-aid kit you assembled before class. Ask:

● **How can we use cotton balls to help someone who's hurt?**

Say: **We can use cotton balls to clean the dirt off a cut before we put a Band-Aid on it.**

Ask:

● **How can we use stickers to help someone who's hurt?**

Say: **We can use stickers to cheer up a friend who's hurt or sick. You can give your friend the sticker and say, "I love you." I put a few stickers on my bag to make it pretty. You can do that too. Before we make our first-aid kits, let's find partners and practice putting Band-Aids on each other.**

Help children find partners. Distribute Band-Aids, then help children open the Band-Aids and put them on their partners. After everyone has applied a Band-Aid, distribute bags, and help children assemble their first-aid kits. Let them choose three or four Band-Aids, a few cotton balls, and several stickers. Set out enough stickers so that children can decorate their bags, too. As they work remind them to love the Lord and love their neighbors as themselves.

Leader Tip

Some children may prefer to put on their own Band-Aids. Or you may want to have children trace their hands on paper and put Band-Aids on their tracings.

While children are assembling their first-aid kits, set up the "dangerous path" for the next activity. Then help the children write their names on their first-aid kits using the permanent marker.

Say: **Good job making your first-aid kits. Your first-aid kit can help you remember our Bible story, and to ❤ Love the Lord . . . and love your neighbor as yourself. Let's play a game that will help us review our Bible story.**

4. Classroom Special
(up to 10 minutes)

Create a "dangerous path" by setting out five or six carpet squares or sheets of construction paper, a chair, two ropes, a table with a sheet or blanket over it, and several throw pillows. Lay out the items in your room according to the diagram below.

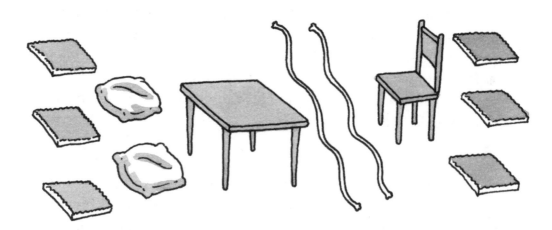

Gather the children at one end of the path, and say: **The man in our story went on a dangerous journey. You can pretend to go on a**

dangerous journey too. Remember, God wants you to 💜 love the Lord . . . and love your neighbor as yourself. So you can take a friend along in case you need help. Can you find a partner?

Help children choose partners, then point out the path, and say: **We'll pretend this is our dangerous path. Be very careful of wild animals and robbers! I'll show you how to go down the dangerous path, then you can take turns going down the path with your partners.**

Go through the course to show the children what to do. As you step on the first carpet squares, say: **These carpet squares are really stones. Don't step off them, or you'll fall into the deep river below.** Climb over the chair, and say: **This is a big, high mountain! Gotta climb over it! Look out for wolves.** As you walk along the rope, say: **Uh-oh! A narrow bridge. Be careful! Don't fall off! There are alligators below!** As you crawl under the table, say: **I found a tunnel through the mountains! I hope there aren't robbers in here!**

When you come to the pillows, say: **More mountains to climb over. They're so high, I'll have to crawl. I don't want to fall off!**

When you reach the last carpet squares, say: **Finally, I'm almost there! I see a few more big stones to hop on.**

Let children take turns following the dangerous path with their partners. Allow a new pair to begin when the previous pair is about halfway through. As children move through the course, remind them of the pretend obstacles they need to overcome. If you have time, let children repeat the course with new partners.

Wrap up the activity by saying: **It looked like you were having fun on the dangerous path. I'm glad you didn't really have to take a dangerous journey like the man in our story did. But Jesus wants you to 💜 love the Lord . . . and love your neighbor as yourself. That's what the nice man in our story did. Let's practice showing love to our neighbors in this class right now!**

5. Classroom Special
(up to 5 minutes)

Set out a small pillow, a stuffed animal, an umbrella, a drinking cup, a coloring book, and crayons. Say: **Jesus wants you to 💜 love the Lord . . . and love your neighbor as yourself. I have some things here that we can use to show our love for others. Let's pretend** your mom is really, really tired. **Can you think of something nice you could do for her, using something on this table?**

Help children choose an item and explain how they could use it to help their moms. For example, they might offer her the pillow so she could rest or use the drinking cup to get her a cool drink of water.

Continue with the following situations. After you read each situation, help children choose an item and explain how they'd use it to help.

- **Your baby brother is crying.**
- **Your big sister is sick in bed, she's thirsty, and your mom is on the phone.**
- **Your grandma is visiting and has to go to the store in the rain.**
- **Your friend comes over to play and wants to color a picture.**

After you've read all the situations, say: **I can tell you're learning to love the Lord . . . and love your neighbor as yourself. Now let's practice helping while we make our snack.**

6. Snack Time
(up to 12 minutes)

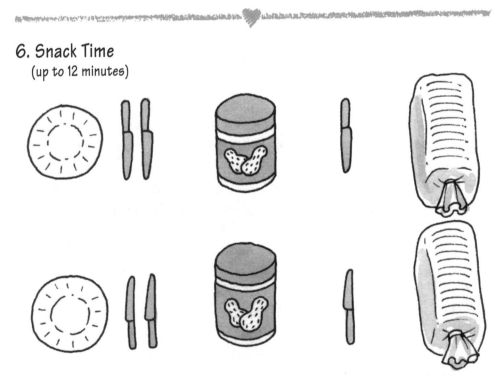

Set out the bags of sliced bread, plastic knives, jars or bowls of peanut butter, and paper plates, as shown above.

Have children wash their hands and then line up on both sides of the table. Say: **God wants you to** ♥ **love the Lord . . . and love your neighbor as yourself. We're going to work together to make our snack today. We're all going to help make peanut butter sandwiches. Remember to be good neighbors and help each other. After you do your part, pass the sandwich to the person next to you.**

Divide up the snack-making tasks so each child gets to do something. For example, you might assign the following tasks:

- removing slices of bread from the bag
- spreading peanut butter on the bread
- putting a second slice of bread on top of the peanut butter
- cutting the sandwiches in half
- cutting the half-sandwiches into quarters
- putting the quarter-sandwiches on plates

As children work, point out that each person is doing a special and important job. Praise children for being good neighbors and helping each other.

Leader Tip

If you have more than fourteen children in your class, set up more than one snack-assembly area. If you have fewer than seven children, combine some of the tasks.

When children have made enough sandwiches for everyone, have them sit down. As you hand out sandwiches and half-full cups of juice or water, have children pass the snacks down the line until everyone is served. As children eat their snacks, say: **Remember to** ♥ **love the Lord . . . and love your neighbor as yourself. You all did a great job of being good neighbors and helping one another!**

7. Closing
(up to 5 minutes)

Lead the children in singing the song from the Sing-Along Start Up, "Love Your Neighbor," to the tune of "Frère Jacques." As you sing, add the actions in parentheses.

Love Your Neighbor

Love the Lord *(point up)*,
And love your neighbor *(hug someone next to you)*
As yourself, as yourself. *(Hug yourself.)*
Love the Lord first *(point up)*
Then your neighbor next. *(Hug someone.)*
Jesus says, Jesus says. *(Point up toward heaven.)*

After you finish the song, close with a prayer similar to this one: "Dear God, thank you for being our friend and for helping us to be good neighbors. Help us to remember to help others by being kind. We want to ♥ love the Lord and love our neighbors as ourselves. Amen."

Give children an opportunity to pray if they want to. Remind them to take their first-aid kits with them when they leave. Encourage them to use their first-aid kits to show kindness this week.

Lost and Found

(Luke 15:1-7)

♥ **God's Message:** "The Lord loves us very much."

(Psalm 117:2a)

Jesus drew criticism from the Pharisees because sinners and tax collectors were drawn to his teaching of God's love and forgiveness. Instead of sending these sinners away, Jesus welcomed them and even ate with them. In response to the Pharisees' attack, Jesus told the parable of the lost sheep. Jesus closed the parable by saying that there's more rejoicing in heaven over one sinner who repents than over ninety-nine righteous people who do not need to repent.

Little children face big worries. They worry that they may be lost like the sheep in Jesus' story, that something terrible will happen to their parents, or that they might do something so bad that their parents will stop loving them. Use this lesson to teach your preschoolers that God cares for them just as the watchful shepherd cares for his sheep and that no matter what they do, God will always love them.

💜 Preparation 💜

You'll need a Bible, photocopies of the "Hide and Sheep" handout (p. 95), scissors, white glue, craft sticks, markers, a bag of confetti or ribbon scraps, and a paper cup for each child.

Before class, cut out the sheep from the handout. Hide the large sheep in preparation for the Bible Story. You'll need one small sheep for each child.

For Snack Time, you'll need instant vanilla-pudding mix, milk, banana slices, paper cups, and spoons. Before class, prepare the pudding according to the package directions. Place several banana slices in the bottom of each paper cup, then cover the bananas with pudding. Prepare a pudding cup for each child.

💜 The Lesson 💜

1. Sing-Along Start-Up
(up to 5 minutes)

Ask:

● **Who loves you?**

Say: **Lots and lots and lots of people love you—including me! Today we're going to learn that 💜 the Lord loves us very much. We'll have fun hearing a Bible story that tells how much God loves us. Before our story, let's learn a happy song about God's love.**

Sing the following song to the tune of "Bingo." Sing the song several times until children know the words.

The Lord Loves Us Very Much

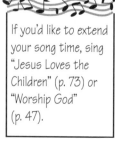

If you'd like to extend your song time, sing "Jesus Loves the Children" (p. 73) or "Worship God" (p. 47).

The great big God who made the world
Cares for little children.
The Lord loves us so very much.
The Lord loves us so very much.
The Lord loves us so very much.
The Bible tells me so.

2. The Bible Story

(up to 10 minutes)

Open your Bible to Luke 15:1-7, and show the passage to the children.

Say: **This is a story that Jesus told about a shepherd and his sheep.**

Ask:

- **What sound does a sheep make?**
- **Who takes care of sheep?**

Say: **Shepherds take good care of their sheep. They lead the sheep to cool water and soft, green grass. They make sure wolves and lions and bears stay away.**

Let's pretend that I'm the shepherd in Jesus' story and all of you are the sheep. Have children get down on their hands and knees and scatter around the room. **One day a shepherd took his sheep to a beautiful hillside where they could eat green grass and drink water from a cool stream. When evening came, the shepherd gathered all his sheep and counted them one by one.**

Walk around the room and "herd" the children. Have them crawl to the middle of the room and sit down. Count each child as he or she joins the group.

Say: **The shepherd counted one, two, three, four, five, six, seven, eight, nine, ten. He kept counting all the way up to ninety-seven, ninety-eight, ninety-nine. And that was the last sheep he could find. There were supposed to be one hundred sheep. One sheep was missing!**

Ask:

- **What do you think the shepherd did when he found that one of his sheep was gone?**

Say: **The shepherd was so worried that he left all the other sheep and went to look for the sheep that was lost. Do you know what? There's a lost sheep somewhere in our classroom. Why don't you help me find it?**

Have children help you hunt for the sheep picture. When someone finds it, have the children cheer.

Say: **The shepherd was so happy when he found the little lost sheep! He picked it up and cuddled it and carried it over his shoulders. Then he called out to his friends and neighbors: "Look! My sheep was lost, but now I've found it. Come celebrate with me."**

Just as the shepherd loved and took care of his sheep, God loves us and takes care of us. 🖤 The Lord loves us very much.

---

3. Crafty Creations
(up to 10 minutes)

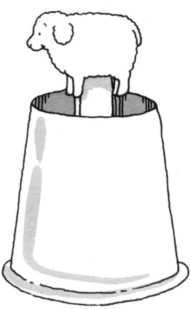

Give each child a small sheep pattern from the "Hide and Sheep" handout. Have each child glue a sheep to the tip of a craft stick. Set out markers, and invite children to decorate their craft sticks, sheep, and paper cups. Encourage children to be careful not to press the cups flat as they color.

Use the craft stick to poke a hole in the bottom of the cup. Demonstrate how to push the sheep puppet through the paper cup and manipulate the puppet with one hand underneath the cup.

Say: **Let's use our sheep puppets to play a game. Hide your sheep inside its cup when I say:**

> **The sheep is lost.**
> **Where can it be?**

Then pop your sheep out of its cup, and answer:

> **I found my sheep.**
> **Hurray! Whoopee!**

Play the game several times, letting different children say the first part of the rhyme.

Leader Tip
To create puppet stages that really look like fields, use paper cups with a floral pattern.

Have children set their sheep puppets in one corner of the room. Then say: 🖤 **The Lord loves us very much. God loves you and promises to take care of you and protect you all the time. Let's see why God is always there to take care of you.**

4. Classroom Special
(up to 10 minutes)

Say: **Let's play another game. You can be the lost sheep, and I'll be the shepherd. I'll cover my eyes and count to twenty while you find hiding places. Then I'll come looking for you. Just like little sheep, you can say, "Baa, baa," to help me find you.**

Cover your eyes, count to twenty, then start calling: **Where are you, little sheep?** As you find each child, have him or her help you hunt for the other children. When everyone has been found, have children gather in a circle. Ask:

- **Did anybody feel scared when we played this game?**
- **What's it like when you really are lost?**
- **Who found you when you were lost?**

Say: **It's nice to know that if you ever get lost, your family will look for you.**

Ask:

- **Why would your family look for you if you were lost?**

Say: **It's scary to be lost. But I've got good news! Even when we're lost, God knows right where we are. God watches over us all the time. ♥ The Lord loves us very much.**

> ### Leader Tip
> On a nice day, consider playing this game outdoors. Be sure you set clear limits as to how far away the children can go to hide.

5. Classroom Special
(up to 10 minutes)

Say: **A good shepherd knows all about his sheep. He knows which one is frisky and playful, which one has the softest little "baa," and which one likes to stay close by his side. Just like a good shepherd, God knows all about us. He made each one of us special. Let's have fun celebrating how much God loves us.**

Choose one child to sit in the middle of the circle. Give the rest of the children handfuls of confetti or ribbon scraps. Have the children gently toss their confetti onto the child in the middle and say, ♥ "The Lord loves you very much."

Choose another child to sit in the middle as the rest of the children pick up the confetti. Continue until each child has been affirmed and showered with confetti. Then have children help you pick up the confetti and throw it away.

As you work together, assure children that even though God made each of us different and special, he loves each of us the same.

6. Snack Time
(up to 10 minutes)

Say: **Thanks for your good work picking up all that confetti! Now I have a special treat for you!** Give each child a cup of prepared pudding and a spoon, and say: **There may be something hiding in the bottom of your pudding. You'll have to search for it carefully, just as the shepherd in our story searched for his lost sheep.**

As the children enjoy their hidden treats, ask questions such as "How is God like a good shepherd?" or "Who can tell about a special time God watched over you?"

Say: **Because ♥ the Lord loves us very much, he's always watching over us. Let's thank God for loving us.**

7. Closing
(up to 5 minutes)

Give the children their puppets and cups. Say: **Let's hold our sheep puppets as we thank God for his love.**

Pray: **God, we thank you for loving us. The Bible tells us that you love us the way a shepherd loves his sheep. You make sure we have plenty to eat and drink. You watch over us all the time. Thank you for being our Good Shepherd. Amen.**

Encourage children to use their sheep puppets to retell the Bible story at home.

Hide and Sheep

A Great Big Picnic

(John 6:1-14)

♥ **God's Message:** "Do many good things with the help of Christ."

(Philippians 1:11a)

What a thrill it must have been for the boy who offered his small lunch to see it miraculously multiplied to feed a crowd of thousands! Though the lunch was totally inadequate to meet the need, Jesus honored the boy's faith. And hurray for Andrew, the disciple who saw the potential in a child's small gift and brought that child to Jesus!

Preschoolers love to have their efforts and accomplishments affirmed. Expressions such as "What a big boy!" or "What a big girl!" always bring proud smiles. Your children will love today's story of how a little boy helped Jesus when grown-ups couldn't. Use this lesson to teach children that even though they're little, God has important things for them to do!

♥ Preparation ♥

You'll need a Bible, a loaf of French bread, a grocery sack, a basket of crackers, newspapers, paint shirts, large sheets of white construction paper, tempera paint, paintbrushes, a sheet or blanket, a popcorn popper, unpopped popcorn, and oil (if needed). Before class, put the loaf of French bread in the grocery sack.

For Snack Time, you'll need a large mixing bowl, a wooden spoon, and four or five different snack-mix items (such as cereal rings, chocolate chips, small pretzels, raisins, or small marshmallows). You'll also need a paper cup for each child. Before class, fill each child's cup with one of the snack-mix ingredients.

♥ The Lesson ♥

1. Sing-Along Start-Up
(up to 5 minutes)

Say: **Today we're going learn about a boy who shared his lunch with Jesus.**

Ask:

● **When have you shared something with a friend?**

● **How did your friend feel when you shared?**

Say: **It's good to share things with others. Sharing isn't always easy, but with Jesus' help, we can do it. Jesus will always help us do good things. Let's learn a song about that.**

Sing the following song to the tune of "Eency, Weency Spider." Sing the song several times until children know the words.

Do Many Good Things

♥ Do many good things
With the help of Christ.
Do many good things
With the help of Christ.
Do many good things
With the help of Christ.
For this is God's message
To you and to me!

If you'd like to extend your song time, sing "God Made Us All to Do Good Works" (p. 32) or "Love Your Neighbor" (p. 81).

Say: **Let's bring out our Bible now and hear about a boy who did good things when he shared with Jesus.**

---

2. The Bible Story
(up to 8 minutes)

Gather the children in the story area, and have them sit down. Set the basket of crackers and the grocery sack holding the French bread out of sight nearby.

Open your Bible to John 6, show the passage to the children, and say: **One day Jesus was teaching a great big crowd of people.** Ask:
● **Have you ever been in a big crowd? Where?**

Continue: **The Bible tells us that more than five thousand people were listening to Jesus. That's a lot of people! Let's count by thousands together. One thousand, two thousand, three thousand, four thousand, five thousand. Very good!**

That big crowd of people had been listening to Jesus teach all day long. They got tired and hungry. Show me what you look like when you're tired and hungry.

Jesus asked his close friends, "Where can we buy enough food for all these people?" His friend Philip answered, "We would have to work a whole month to buy enough bread for this crowd—and then everyone would get only a little piece!"

Andrew, another friend of Jesus, said: "There's a little boy here. He has a lunch with five little loaves of bread and two fish. But that's not enough to feed all these people."

Show children the basket of crackers, then continue: **The little boy's lunch might have been as much as this basket of crackers. Is this enough food to feed all the people in our church? No, it's not. And the boy's lunch wasn't enough to feed five thousand people. But the little boy must have been very excited to see what Jesus would do with his lunch. Jesus took the lunch, thanked God for it, then started giving bread and fish to everyone.**

Pass the crackers to the children as you say: **And do you know what? As Jesus handed out the little boy's lunch, something very special happened!** Take out the loaf of French bread, break off pieces, and hand them out. **The bread and fish never ran out! In fact, there were twelve baskets of food left over.**

I brought an extra loaf of bread to make sure we'd have enough for our class, but Jesus didn't have to! He just kept on passing out the little boy's lunch! The more he gave, the more there was to give. All the people ate until they were full. It was a miracle!

Put any leftover bread away, and say: **Think of how the people felt that day. They were so hungry their tummies were growling, then Jesus gave them all the food they could eat.**

Ask:

● **What important thing did the little boy in our story do?**

● **What if the boy hadn't shared his lunch?**

Say: **Jesus used the little boy's lunch to feed five thousand people! That's pretty special! I know another thing that's special— Jesus can use you to do good things, just as he used the boy in our story.**

Ask:

● **What are some good things you can do?**

You might suggest responses such as sharing toys, giving hugs, playing with a younger brother or sister, or helping set the table.

Then say: **Those are great ideas! You're never too little to do important things for God. Remember, you can  do many good things with the help of Christ.**

3. Crafty Creations
(up to 10 minutes)

Cover a table with newspapers. Give each child a sheet of white construction paper. Set out containers of tempera paint and paintbrushes, then help children fold their papers in half. Fold your own sheet of paper in half, open it, and paint a simple "blob" design on one half of the paper.

Say: **God made each one of us special.** Refold the paper, and press the halves together. **When we give what we have to Jesus, he makes it into something special.**

Open the paper to reveal the mirrored print of the design you painted. Show it to the children, and say: **See how special my painting is now? Jesus can take the little things we do and make them extra special. That's why we can  do many good things with the help of Christ. Now I'd like to see your special pictures!**

Have children put on paint shirts, and let the children paint designs on their papers then fold and press them to make prints. Set the finished designs aside to dry.

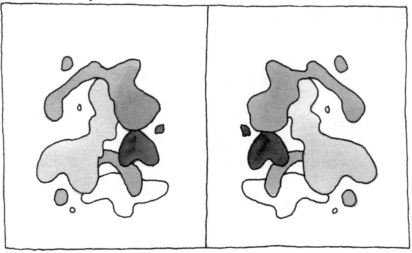

4. Classroom Special
(up to 10 minutes)

Spread a sheet or blanket on the floor, and have children sit around the edges of it. Put a popcorn popper in the middle of the sheet, and plug it in. As the popper heats up, hold up a few kernels of unpopped popcorn, and ask:

● **Does anyone know what this is?**

● **Would it taste good if we ate it like this?**

Say: **Unpopped popcorn is too hard—we'd hurt our teeth if we tried to eat it. But when these little popcorn kernels get popped, they become warm and delicious.**

> **Leader Tip**
>
> If your popcorn popper requires oil, don't begin heating the popper until after the children have dropped in their popcorn. That way, no one will get burned if the oil splashes.

Have each child drop a few kernels of popcorn into the popper. Leave the top off the popper. As you wait for the popcorn to start popping, say: **The boy in our story gave Jesus a little lunch—like a handful of popcorn kernels. Then Jesus turned it into something wonderful, just like what's happening to our popcorn now! Jesus can take the good things we do and turn them into something bigger and better. Let's watch how our popcorn turns into something bigger and better.**

Lead children in clapping and saying, "Yea, Jesus!" as the popcorn pops. Then let children gobble up the popcorn as you remove the popper and set it aside, out of children's reach. Remind children that they can  do many good things with the help of Christ.

5. Classroom Special
(up to 10 minutes)

Have children gather in a group on their hands and knees. Say: **I'm going to cover you with this big sheet and make you look like a big loaf of bread. When you hear me say, "Feed all the people," crawl out from underneath the sheet. When everyone's out, I'll pick up the sheet and say, "Loaf of bread!" Then you can crawl back under the sheet.**

Play the game two or three times, then have children sit on the sheet and take three deep breaths. Say: **Jesus started with a little bit of bread, then made it feed all the people! And it all started with a little boy's lunch. Jesus can use little people like you to do big things. Remember, you can** do many good things with the help of Christ.

6. Snack Time
(up to 10 minutes)

Set a large mixing bowl on a table. Gather the children around you. Give each child a paper cup containing one of the snack-mix ingredients. Instruct children not to nibble their snacks just yet. Ask:

● **Is the snack in your cup enough to feed everyone in this class?**

- Now look at the snack in your neighbor's cup. Is it different from yours, or is it the same?
- What if you want the kind of snack your neighbor has?

Point out the mixing bowl, and say: **Remember, God wants us to ♥ do many good things with the help of Christ. Let's all pour our snacks into this big bowl. We can mix it up and share a little bit of everything with each other!**

After children pour their snacks into the bowl, let them take turns stirring the mix with a wooden spoon. Have each child scoop out a cup of snack mix and give it to someone else. When everyone has been served, ask a volunteer to give thanks for the snack. Then invite everyone to munch.

7. Closing
(up to 7 minutes)

Have children sit in a circle on the floor. Say: **All of you in this class may be little, but I know you can do good things for Jesus. If you think that's true, clap your hands and say, "Hurray!"**

Walk behind the children, and touch one child's head. Say: **When I touch your head and say, "**(Name of child) **may be little," you stand up and say, "but I'll do good things for Jesus!" Let's try that.**

Repeat the phrase, and let the child stand and respond. Then walk around the circle and touch each child's head. If some children are too shy to stand up and repeat the phrase, help everyone say, "He (or she) will do good things for Jesus."

When everyone has been affirmed, close with the following prayer: **"Thank you, God, that you can use these wonderful children even though they're very young. Help us all to ♥ do many good things with the help of Christ. Please show us good things we can do this week. Amen."**

Remind children to take their special pictures home.

Alive Again!

(Mark 15:12-39; 16:1-13)

♥ **God's Message:** "Jesus has risen from the dead."

(Matthew 28:7a)

To pay for the sins of the world, Jesus willingly suffered a cruel execution usually reserved for hardened criminals. This is a sad and frightening story for young children. It's important to help them understand that Jesus died for us because he loves us and that he rose again in three days because he is more powerful than anyone or anything.

Preschoolers know what it means to do something wrong. They make choices every day, such as whether to obey or disobey, whether to be kind or unkind, and whether to be caring or selfish. In this lesson, children will hear that Jesus died so we can be forgiven for the wrong things we do. They'll learn that Jesus rose from the dead so we can live with him in heaven someday. Use this lesson to help children discover that Jesus is alive today.

♥ Preparation ♥

You'll need a Bible, paint shirts, construction paper, a nine-by-thirteen-inch cake pan, cups of tempera paint and one cup of water, a golf ball, a marker, plastic spoons, a grocery sack, and a helium balloon and a regular balloon of similar size and color. Before class, tie a string to each balloon, then put the balloons inside the grocery sack. You'll also need a balloon or crepe paper streamer for each child, old newspapers, and a roll of masking tape.

For Snack Time, you'll need chocolate milk, paper cups, plastic spoons, and a bowl of marshmallows.

Leader Tip

To add a festive touch, bring in a bouquet of helium balloons, and tie them to a chair as a decoration. Have one balloon for each child, and make sure the strings are long enough for you to reach them when they float to the ceiling. Keep the balloons together until you're ready to use them during the closing activity.

♥ The Lesson ♥

1. Sing-Along Start-Up
(up to 5 minutes)

Say: **I'm happy because today I get to tell you the happiest story in the whole Bible.** Let the children guess which story you're talking about. Then say: **Today we're going to learn what happened on the very first Easter. To get ready for that story, let's learn a happy song!**

Sing the following song to the tune of "The Mulberry Bush." Sing the song several times until children know the words.

Jesus Has Risen

♥ Jesus has risen from the dead,
From the dead, from the dead.
Jesus has risen from the dead.
He is alive!

Will you love Jesus? Yes, we will!
Yes, we will! Yes, we will!
Will you love Jesus? Yes, we will!
He is alive!

If you'd like to extend your song time, sing "God Is With Us" (p. 56) or "Jesus Loves the Children" (p. 73).

Say: ♥ **Jesus has risen from the dead, and that's something to** celebrate! We can be happy because Jesus is alive today. Let's bring out our Bible and hear how Jesus died and rose again.

2. The Bible Story
(up to 10 minutes)

Gather the children around you. If you tied helium balloons to a chair, sit on that chair as you tell the story. Open your Bible to Mark 15–16, and show the section to the children. Say:

Jesus traveled all over the countryside, teaching people about God's love. He asked people to stop doing mean things and start doing what God wanted them to do. What are some things God wants us to do?

Some people were mean and selfish. They were angry that so many people followed Jesus and believed in him. They wanted to get rid of Jesus, so they sent soldiers to arrest him. The leaders took Jesus to the governor and said, "This man is bad—he must be killed."

The governor's name was Pilate. He had to decide if Jesus had done anything wrong. He asked Jesus lots of questions and found out that Jesus hadn't done anything wrong.

Pilate asked the people if he should let Jesus go. "No!" the people shouted. Pilate knew Jesus hadn't done anything wrong, but he was afraid of the angry crowd. So he told the soldiers to take Jesus and hang him on a cross.

Soon Jesus died. His friends and followers were very, very sad. They knew Jesus hadn't done anything wrong and didn't deserve to die. A friend laid Jesus' body in a tomb and rolled a big, heavy stone in front of the opening.

Three days later, three women went to the tomb to put sweet-smelling spices on Jesus' body. On their way they said to each other: "How will we ever move the stone away from the door? How will we get in?" But when they got there, the stone had been rolled away! An angel in a shining, white robe said: "Don't be afraid. I know you're looking for Jesus. He has risen from the dead. He is not here. Go, and tell his followers."

The women ran to tell Jesus' other friends that he was alive. And do you know what? Jesus is alive today! He's always with us. Let's all say, "Hurray for Jesus!"

Lead children in cheering for Jesus, then ask:
- **How would you feel if you saw an angel?**
- **What do you think Jesus' friends said when they found out Jesus was alive?**

Take the helium balloon and the regular balloon out of the grocery sack. Hold them both by their knots, and say: ♥ **Jesus has risen from the dead, so I've brought some balloons to celebrate! What do you think will happen if I let these balloons go?**

Let children respond, then let go of both balloons. Point to the helium balloon, and say: **This balloon rose to the ceiling because it's special. It's filled with helium, and that makes it float. Jesus is special too. Because Jesus is God's Son, he's powerful enough to rise from the dead. Just as our helium balloon rose to the ceiling, Jesus rose from the dead then went up to heaven to live with God. If we believe in Jesus, we can live with him in heaven someday too.**

Now let's make a special craft to remind us of this very special story.

3. Crafty Creations
(up to 7 minutes)

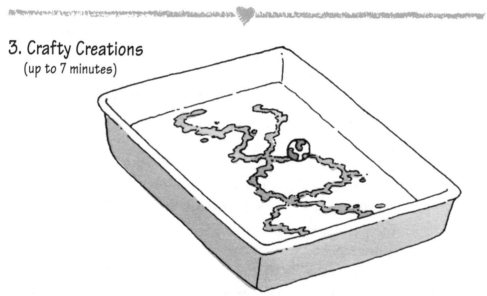

Cover a table with old newspapers. Set out cups of tempera paint and the cup of water, plastic spoons, a nine-by-thirteen-inch cake pan, a marker, and construction paper. Help the children put on paint shirts.

Say: **When the women went to Jesus' tomb, they discovered that the stone had been rolled away and Jesus was alive. We're going to make special rolling-stone paintings to help us remember that** ♥ **Jesus has risen from the dead.**

Hold up a golf ball. Say: **This golf ball will be our "stone." We'll take turns dipping the golf ball in the paint and rolling it around to make pretty designs on paper. You'll each get to dip and roll the golf-ball stone five times. While you're waiting for a turn, you can say a fun cheer. It goes like this:**

One roll,
Two rolls,
Three, four, five.
We know Jesus is alive!

Leader Tip

If your church doesn't have paint shirts, you can make your own by cutting head and arm holes in paper grocery sacks.

Let's practice once together.

Lead children in saying the cheer, then place a sheet of paper inside the cake pan. Show children how to dip the golf ball into a cup of paint, then place the golf ball in the cake pan and gently tip the cake pan from side to side. Point out the interesting designs the ball makes as it rolls over the paper. Rinse off the ball in the cup of water, dip it in a second color of paint, and roll the ball over the paper again. Let each child dip and roll the ball five times, making sure to rinse it off between colors, as you lead other children in saying the cheer. Help the children use the marker to write their names on their paintings. Set the completed paintings aside to dry.

4. Classroom Special
(up to 10 minutes)

Say: **You made beautiful rolling-stone paintings! Now let's play a popping-up game to remind us that ♥ Jesus has risen from the dead. Scatter around the room, and squat down. I'll walk around and sing the song we learned during our Sing-Along Start-Up. When I touch you on the head, jump up, hold my hand, and join me in singing the song. Then we'll touch someone else, and that person will join us. When you hear the words "He is alive!" jump high in the air and say, "Yea, Jesus!"**

Walk or skip around the room and tap children on the head as you sing "Jesus Has Risen" to the tune of "The Mulberry Bush."

Jesus Has Risen

♥ Jesus has risen from the dead *(tap a child's head)*,
From the dead *(tap another child's head)*,
From the dead. *(Tap another child's head.)*
Jesus has risen from the dead. *(Tap another child's head.)*
He is alive! *(Jump up and say, "Yea, Jesus!")*

Repeat the verse until everyone has joined hands and is singing with you. Then form a circle, and walk around as you sing the last verse together.

Will you love Jesus? Yes, we will!
Yes, we will! Yes, we will!
Will you love Jesus? Yes, we will!
He is alive! *(Jump up and say, "Yea, Jesus!")*

5. Classroom Special
(up to 12 minutes)

Leader Tip

Have a damp towel or washcloth on hand for cleaning newsprint ink off the children's hands.

Say: **That was a fun game! Who's ready to play another game?** Give each child one or two sheets of newspaper. Show children how to crumple their papers to form a large ball. Help them wrap masking tape around their paper balls to keep them from coming apart.

Say: **We're going to pretend that these paper balls are stones like the one that was in front of Jesus' tomb.** Have everyone stand on one side of the room. Say: **Put your stone on the floor in front of you. When I say, ♥ "Jesus has risen from the dead!" use your feet to roll your stone to the other side of the room. Then come back to this side. Ready? ♥ Jesus has risen from the dead!**

When children have moved their stones across the room and returned, ask:

● **Who would like to tell a new way to move the stone?** Children might suggest pushing the stones with their noses, rolling the stones with their hands, or carrying the stones and hopping. Let several children have turns telling new ways to move the stones then calling out, "Jesus has risen from the dead!"

After several rounds, say: **All this stone-rolling is making me thirsty. Let's put our stones away and have a refreshing treat.**

6. Snack Time
(up to 7 minutes)

Give each child a cup of chocolate milk and a plastic spoon. Set out a bowl of marshmallows.

Hold up a cup of chocolate milk, and ask: **What will happen if I put a marshmallow in my cup of milk?**

Let children respond. Then put a marshmallow in your cup, and say: **See? The marshmallow rises to the top. Even if I take a spoon and push the marshmallow down, it still comes back up. It makes me remember that Jesus didn't stay down in the tomb.**  **Jesus has risen from the dead!**

Let children drop marshmallows in their chocolate milk. Encourage them to push the marshmallows down with their spoons and watch them float back up to the top. Then enjoy the treat together.

7. Closing
(up to 5 minutes)

If you brought enough helium balloons for each child to have one, hold up the balloons, and say: **I have a balloon for each of you to take home. But first let's repeat God's message to us. When I hand you a balloon, say,**  **"Jesus has risen from the dead."**

When each child has a balloon, say: **You did that so well! Let's say it**

Leader Tip

If you didn't bring helium balloons, give children plain balloons or colored crepe paper streamers. Have children wave their balloons or streamers as you sing "Jesus Has Risen," then close with prayer.

one more time, this time all together, nice and loud. Then we'll let our balloons float up to the ceiling to remind us that Jesus rose from the dead. After we let go of the balloons, we'll say a prayer. Then I'll pull the balloons back down and help you tie them to your wrists.

Lead children in saying: ♥ Jesus has risen from the dead, as they release their balloons. Have children look up at the balloons as you pray: **Dear God, thank you for sending Jesus to die on the cross for us. The brightly colored balloons remind us of how happy we are that Jesus rose from the dead and is alive today. Help us to follow Jesus this week. Amen.**

Tie the balloons to children's wrists as they leave. Remind children to take their rolling-stone paintings home.